D1482122

ARMS AND ARMOR

War has always held a powerful, even if self-destructive, fascination for man. It has probably occupied more time and taken a larger share of effort and wealth than any other of his endeavors. Although war has always been a sordid business, time does soften its impact and gives it a false image of glamour and excitement. No period is more prone to be so treated than the Middle Ages with its knights and their gaily bedecked horses. The study of their armor is a fascinating one, although it is but one stage in the long sequence of discoveries and developments that has led from the leather cap of the ancient Middle East right up to the sophisticated, armored fighting vehicle of today.

This book shows how the changes in arms and armor have been the result of a constant struggle between the armorer and the weapon-maker. Each improvement in weapon design evoked some response from the armorer, who increased the thickness of plate or added an extra glancing surface. Today the struggle is basically the same, although in place of an armored knight there is a giant tank and the archer has been superseded by an anti-tank gunner. The once knightly sword has now become largely an ornament or uniform accessory, and its place has been taken by weapons far more terrible than the early swordsmiths could ever have conceived in their wildest dreams.

F.W.

A GROSSET ALL-COLOR GUIDE

ARMS AND ARMOR

BY FREDERICK WILKINSON
Illustrated by John H. Batchelor and Arthur Gay

GROSSET & DUNLAP
A NATIONAL GENERAL COMPANY
Publishers ▪ New York

THE GROSSET ALL-COLOR GUIDE SERIES
SUPERVISING EDITOR . . . GEORG ZAPPLER

Board of Consultants

399
c 3

CONTENTS

ANCIENT WORLD

Introduction of metal

Copper was the first metal to be used by man. This tremendous leap forward was apparently first taken in Anatolia. Its use was known to the Egyptians by the beginning of the fourth millenium, although by then it had been employed elsewhere for a thousand years. Knowledge of this technique spread slowly, probably reaching Europe via Greece and the Balkans. Copper axes and daggers were, however, too soft to hold an edge for very long and therefore needed frequent sharpening.

But copper could be hardened by adding a small amount of tin, and the alloy became known as bronze. Only a small percentage of tin was needed; for daggers and swords only about two percent was required. Not only was bronze harder, but it was also easier to cast than pure copper.

Iron was first smelted in Asia Minor, and examples of iron objects dating from 3000 B.C. have been excavated there. The Hittites first made steel in large quantity around 1500 B.C. It was probably because this nation had strong iron swords that it was able to conquer so much of the Near East.

Daggers from Ur and Anatolia (c. 2500 B.C.). Axes from Egypt (c. 2000 B.C.).

4

Wooden shields from Egyptian tombs (c. 2000 B.C.). Crescent-shaped, cutting-and-slashing swords typical of the sort used by Egyptians and Sumerians (c. 1900 B.C.).

Egyptian sword and shield

Egyptian battle shields were of leather-covered wood, but when metal became more plentiful a boss was added near the top to afford extra strength. Shields for nobles were decorated by adding fur, that of Tutankhamen was covered with antelope skin. Tomb paintings show workshops with craftsmen producing these simple shields, and surviving examples are not uncommon. When not in use, the shield could be carried on the shoulder by means of a long, leather strap.

Swords were a practical impossibility when only flint was available—they would have been too heavy and fragile. They did not appear until the discovery of metals. Early ones had a straight, tapered blade and were intended essentially as a stabbing weapon. The hilt was secured to the blade by a series of rivets, and the pommel or weight at the top of the grip was often carved into attractive shapes. Around 2500 B.C. the first of the slashing swords was developed and took the form of a curved sickle-shaped blade. This sword, called a *khopesh,* was a popular Egyptian weapon and, indeed, became the symbol of the pharaoh's power. Axes were also popular weapons; the head was lashed to the shaft or fitted on by means of a socket.

Early warfare

With the urban civilization of Asia Minor, the first organized armies were brought into being. Large numbers of men were led into battle as a unit instead of just indulging in a series of individual, haphazard, hand-to-hand combats. Armies included chariots and cavalry in addition to foot soldiers. If the wall paintings of the period are to be accepted at face value, Egyptian troops were well provided, but in comparison with such countries as Sumer their type of warfare was rather primitive.

Although the Sumerian soldier wore a simple form of metal-studded leather cape and a leather or metal helmet, certainly by 2800 B.C. the Egyptian soldier still had only his shield for defense. Most of the infantry carried a shield which was at first simply an animal skin stretched over a wooden frame. Later it was made rectangular and then given a curved top. Many of the shields were quite small, presumably designed to protect only the head and body. Some circular shields are shown on Egyptian wall paintings, but these were apparently used only by foreign auxiliaries.

Flakes of flint were sometimes fitted to simple handles to form daggers, while shaped pieces of rock fitted onto wooden handles made crude but serviceable maces.

The axe shown on the carving must represent the axes with socketed, cast bronze heads used by the Sumerians. The example on the left is decorated with gold (c. 2000 B.C.).

Egyptian weapons

Even when metal came into general use, flint and stone were not abandoned completely; they were easily obtainable and continued to be used for the more commonplace weapons. Mace-heads were frequently just a round piece of stone roughly shaped into flanges, with a hole painstakingly drilled through the center to take a wooden shaft. Flint blades were also fashioned and fitted into hilts which were often carved into attractive shapes and patterns with high relief.

Even when metal blades replaced those of stone, the minerals were still employed for hilts and for their decorative qualities. Egyptians made considerable use of the bow, both the simple arc form and the double-curved type, and the arrow-heads were still made of flint. Much Egyptian metal was imported from Sinai and Persia and was, therefore, quite expensive.

Light chariots were a feature of Egyptian cavalry. This example, decorated with gold, was buried with its owner in the fifteenth century B.C. Chariots often carried an archer, and here a noble holds a double-convex bow and a bunch of reed arrows.

Chariots

Although the Egyptians were noted for their use of chariots, these came originally from Canaan and appear on stone carvings there as early as 3000 B.C. A typical Egyptian chariot was extremely light. By about 1400 B.C. it had acquired its characteristic form, with two four-spoked wheels, the rims covered with leather, mounted on a single axle which was fixed at the rear of the simple, light body. From the center of the body projected a shaft about five feet long, at the end of which was a double yoke to fit over the horses' shoulders, with straps passing around the front of the horses' necks to secure them to the chariot. Many were made as two-man vehicles, holding a charioteer who looked after the horses and an archer or spearman who concentrated on the fighting. Extra arrows or javelins were normally carried in a quiver mounted permanently on the side of the chariot. The body was simply a wooden framework covered with leather or equally lightweight material, and on the royal chariot the sides are shown as being decorated in high relief.

From about 1400 B.C. the wheel was strengthened; a six-spoked type was adopted and remained more or less standard for all chariots. The horses were frequently richly bedecked, their backs covered with a brightly decorated cloth. Chariots were also used for hunting and conventional transport.

Assyrian armies

From carvings found on monuments it seems certain that the Assyrian chariot was larger and heavier than that of the Egyptians, and that their armies were far better equipped. Chariot wheels were six-spoked with wide, thick rims, and the carriage was large enough to hold three people—a driver, an archer, and a third man whose job seems to have been to guard the others with a round shield. The Assyrians developed larger, more complex vehicles like mobile battering rams. In addition to the chariots there were large bodies of cavalry, archers, spearmen, and slingmen. As well as their main weapon, most soldiers also carried a short, straight-bladed sword. Although mail was also used, most wore a protective tunic reaching to the knees or ankles, made of overlapping plates presumably attached to a leather garment.

Assyrian soldiers carried spears and wicker shields and wore various forms of armor, as well as crested helmets. Their chariots were heavier than the Egyptian variety, capable of carrying up to three men.

CLASSICAL WORLD

Early Greek warrior

Greek armorers and weapon-smiths produced pieces that were not only technically very competent but also aesthetically pleasing. They made great use of bronze for their armor, often employing the springiness of the metal to hold the pieces in position on the body.

There were many individual combats, and Greek epics abound with accounts of the combats and of the armor of the combatants. The protagonists might well have worn armor or have fought practically naked except for helmet and shield. Mycenaen helmets of around 1500 B.C. were elaborate, having a leather cap covered with bands of boars' tusks, alternate rows pointing in opposite directions. The large shields were made of leather and wood, with metal reinforcing. Some were like the Egyptians', straight-sided with a curved top, whereas others were like a violin in outline.

Later on, spearmen were organized into a solid phalanx, with 18-foot pikes, or *sarissa*, and a small buckler.

(Above) some hoplites fought nearly naked, but all carried the large, circular shield held by the strap at the rim.
(Opposite top) a remarkable set of bronze plate armor dating from the late fifteenth century B.C., found at Dendra near Mycenae *(see page 15)*.
(Bottom left) a reconstruction of a Mycenaen helmet, composed of strips of boar tusk fastened to a leather foundation cap.
(Bottom right) Bronze Age swords from Mycenae, intended as slashing weapons. They vary in length from 20 to 30 inches.

Earlier spears were for thrusting, leaving close combat to be decided by swords. Bows were apparently too weak to give arrows power to penetrate shield or armor. Heavily armed and armored Greeks were able to overcome lighter armed opponents, such as the Persians and the Egyptians, and as a result armor gradually became heavier and more elaborate.

Greek armor

Perhaps the most characteristic helmet of ancient Greece is that known as the Corinthian. It was first illustrated on vases and bronze figures about 700 B.C. and was soon widely adopted. It reached down to the shoulder and completely enclosed the head except for a T-shaped opening leaving the nose, eyes, and mouth clear, although a nasal, or projecting, bar over the nose, offered further protection here. The entire helmet was hammered out of a single piece of bronze—no mean feat! Surviving examples of the Corinthian have a series of holes around the rim, which clearly indicate that padding and a lining must normally have been fitted. Another common type was that called Illyrian; it was made in two pieces and joined by a ridge running across the crown of the helmet. Its shape was simpler than that of a Corinthian, and the helmet had pointed cheek-pieces.

Less common than the Illyrian and the conventional

Many hoplites wore the beautifully made and all-enveloping style of helmet usually known as the Corinthian, which appeared as early as 700 B.C.

Far simpler to construct was the Illyrian helmet with its pointed cheek-pieces, for it was made in two pieces which were then joined along the top.

A finely embossed helmet from the Mediterranean island of Crete in a style not unlike the mainland Corinthian, except that it had no nose-guard.

The Chalcidian bronze helmet was less comprehensive than the Corinthian form, for it had spaces cut for the ears, but was otherwise very similar.

Corinthian helmets was that identified as Chalcidian because it appears on pottery so named by archaeologists. It had open spaces for the ears and a simple nasal. A variation of the Corinthian helmet was produced by the craftsmen of Crete, and this form was smaller in size and decorated with high-relief design. Since most of these helmets made it impossible to recognize the wearer, it became the custom to fit the helmet with a crest. Some were of beaten bronze and took the form of 'ears', great, sweeping curves, or simpler shapes; others were fashioned from horsehair.

Body armor was used extensively by the Greeks and ranged from fairly simple arrangements of plates to skillfully shaped corselets fitting closely to the body. From earliest times the Greek warrior used close-fitting, bronze greaves to protect the lower part of his legs.

Greek swords

Greek warriors used many weapons, but the sword was not considered the most important among them. For many years the hoplite with his long spear regarded the sword as a reserve weapon to be used only in the last resort. Swords of Mycenae were made of bronze and had long, thin blades which probably made them unwieldy. Early examples were often inlaid with gold and decorated with ivory. By about 1500 B.C. more unsettled times had produced a practical, short-bladed weapon whose blade was fitted with horned or cruciform projections to serve as a hand-guard. By the sixth century B.C. most troops were carrying a short sword in a sheath below the left arm.

Macedonian infantry carried short stabbing swords, but during the sixth century B.C. a curved, single-edged slashing sword known as the *kopis* was introduced. It somewhat resembled the modern Ghurka *kukri*, with the blade widening

The Boeotian helmet offered protection with minimum inconvenience to sight and hearing.

Long, shaped cheek-pieces distinguished the Thracian helmet from other Greek helmets.

near the top to ensure maximum weight at the cutting point. The *kopis* was used with a slashing stroke delivered from above the left shoulder and was a deadly weapon, as the Spartans demonstrated at Thermopylae.

Late Greek warrior

Many Greeks found that helmets of the Corinthian and Chalcidian shapes interfered with their sight and hearing. Xenophon recommended the type known as Boeotian, which depended on a down-drooping brim for facial protection rather than the nasal and earflaps found on earlier helmets. By the fourth century B.C. most body armors were unlike earlier ones, being close fitting and often embossed with raised representations of muscles. The legs were protected by close-fitting greaves, and some hoplites had extra pieces to protect the ankles and arms.

(*Above left*) a curved, slightly widened blade made the *kopis* a useful slashing weapon.
(*Above right*) many hoplites used a cruciform-shaped sword.
(*Right*) a late Greek warrior equipped for battle in close-fitting conselet, greaves, and helment, holding a shield which bears a typical decoration.

15

Etruscans

Who the Etruscans were and where they came from is almost as much a mystery now as it was in Roman times. Even their language is unlike any other and has defied all efforts at translation. It was most probably from the Orient that they came to settle in Italy, perhaps from Asia Minor. They formed a loose conglomeration of cities, each largely autonomous, and it is from the tombs of cities like Tarquinii and Velutonia that most of our knowledge about the Etruscans has been derived. Ironically, it was the work that the Etruscans put into developing the site of Rome that was responsible for the ascendancy of that town and its citizens, and eventually for the subjugation of Eturia by the Romans themselves. Greeks and Carthaginians both influenced Etruscan development which, in turn, laid the foundations for many later Roman institutions, not least the military might of Imperial Rome.

It seems likely that the Etruscans were essentially a maritime power, but warriors figure frequently in their tomb paintings and on pottery, and a number of examples of their arms and armor have been excavated. They wore a bronze helmet resembling a modern crash helmet and many of the paintings show it fitted with large, impractical crests, but whether these were ever used in battle is open to doubt.

Their body defenses were of the type known as scale armor, which is made up by lacing together overlapping

Roman legionary's bronze helmet with typical peak but lacking cheek-pieces, worn before the first century A.D. (*see page 20*).

A few more elaborate, decorated helmets have survived, but they were primarily parade pieces for they are of very thin metal.

Rome fought the Etruscans for
her existence and later developed her famed legions of pro-
fessional soldiers and officers.

metal plates. This was a simple form of protective garment
which was more effective against slashes than determined
thrusts. It was a style of armor apparently favored by the
Assyrians, and it has been used in a variety of styles throughout the world, including Japan.

Etruscans appear to have relied, like the Greeks, more on
the spear than the sword, and most warriors are depicted
carrying two spears with large, leaf-shaped heads. Swords,
when carried, are shown as short and also leaf-shaped. It is
perhaps no coincidence that the Roman legions relied heavily
on the effect of a barrage of javelins to demoralize the enemy
before advancing with their short swords.

Romans

For many centuries the Roman army was the supreme military force in the Western world; it was efficient, well-trained and, with a few exceptions, well-officered. At first it was essentially a citizens' army, with all Roman citizens being involved. Their equipment and role were determined by wealth. The richest were equipped with shield, breast-plate, greaves, helmet, sword and spear; less wealthy men omitted the breast-plate. Poor men had only a helmet; still poorer men had no armor at all and carried only a spear and sword.

Tactics were based on the legion, apparently introduced in the latter part of the fourth century B.C. In place of the solid phalanx, the troops were arranged in three lines: the *hastati* in front, then the *principes,* and last the *triarii.* Hastati were armed with javelins and spears and carried a large, rectangular wood-and-leather shield, the *scutum;* they also wore body armor. This rank engaged the enemy, but if unsuccessful it retired leaving the *principes,* seasoned, well-trained soldiers, to continue the battle, while the *triarii* knelt and positioned their long spears to form a strong defensive line. If the *principes* failed to break the enemy or were forced to retreat, the rear rank had to complete the task. A small group of cavalry (about 300) was attached to each legion (about 3,000 men). Lack of stirrups limited the effect of cavalry charges.

Organization and tactical use of the legion were to vary over the centuries from the creation of the Republic to the fall of the Empire. There were corresponding changes in weapons, but for many centuries the legionary was equipped with the *gladius* and *pilum,* while wearing body armor and carrying a *scutum.* The *gladius,* which had a blade about two feet long and two inches wide, apparently originated in Spain. The *pilum* was a throwing spear with a small point at the end of a long, soft-iron shaft which, in turn, was fastened to a wooden haft. Once thrown, the spear could not be thrown back, for the iron was easily bent out of shape, from the impact. Mail and scale armor were used, but the *lorica segmentata,* made of carefully designed and cunningly arranged strips of metal, was worn by the majority of the legionaries. Helmets were of bronze, reinforced with iron, with a neck-guard, a peak, and earflaps.

For serious fighting the legionary relied on his short sword (*above*), the *gladius;* his throwing spear (*right*), the *pilum;* and a great shield (*far right*), the *scutum.* For the business of triumphs and parades he had elaborate helmets complete with full face-masks (*below*).

Gauls

Although the Romans fought some battles against semi-naked barbarians, some of their opponents, such as the Gauls, did wear helmets or armor. Their helmets were either functional, with a plain bowl and small peak, or else decorative to an exaggerated point or having a pair of horns and a crest in the shape of a wheel. Their shields were usually oval in shape, but some were rectangular, with a slight waist. From their enemies the Romans learned the use of heavy cavalry and of their long-bladed, double-edged swords fitted with simple hand-guards and wooden or horn grips. Against the mounted bowmen of Asia, such as the Parthians, Roman arms were less effective.

Standard bearers (*right*) always led against the Gauls (*above*).

Gladiators

Bread and circuses were traditionally the means of keeping the mobs of Rome happy, and gladiatorial combats were always popular. Fights were arranged between a wide variety of combatants—men against beasts or dwarfs against women—but it was the trained gladiators who aroused audiences to greatest enthusiasm. *Bestiarii* were made to fight lions, tigers, and many other exotic animals. *Retiarii* used tridents and nets and fought without armor, relying on speed and skill to elude their armored opponents. *Mirmillones* were quite heavily armored, having a large helmet (fitted with a wide peak, a high comb, and a visor which completely covered the face) and armor on the left arm; they carried shields and swords.

The Roman spectacle often included captives using their native weapons, so that a gladiator (*left*) might find himself opposing a Briton with a fine bronze shield as shown here.

The wandering of nations

About A.D. 300 migration of tribes from Asia brought about a complete change of weapons and tactics. Gothic horsemen armed with iron-bound buckler, thrusting spear and long sword (*spatha*) destroyed the Roman legions at Adrianople. At about the same time the Eastern Roman empire also made armored horsemen (*cataphracti*) their main reliance copying arms and armor from their enemies, the Persians. The Huns taught Western Europe the value of lightly armored horse archers, a lesson that was repeated by the Mongols and the Turks a thousand years later. Very few weapons of this period survive, and we must place our reliance on the descriptions of Byzantine authors.

Hun warriors on their small horses.

A group of Gothic warriors,
representative of the barbarian
tribes that destroyed the might of Rome.

SAXONS AND VIKINGS

Saxon warrior

The Saxons came originally from what is now northern Germany and Denmark, and they were raiding the English coast during Roman times. Tradition states that they first came to Britain as mercenaries, hired by an English king to drive back the marauding Picts from the north. However that may be, the Saxons eventually settled in Britain and created their own petty kingdoms, often at war with each other.

Their defensive equipment was a shield, usually round, decorated and strengthened by a metal rim and boss. Those helmets which have survived are almost all of high quality and were certainly the property of rulers and nobles. Some, like that from Sutton Hoo, are conical, with face-guards and neck-guards which are decorated with gilding and silver wire applied to suggest features. Body armor was often of mail, but there is strong evidence to suggest that strips of metal were incorporated with the mail to give extra strength.

Saxon armor as elaborate as the Sutton Hoo helmet was rare.

Saxon weapons

Saxon swords were of basic design and had a simple hilt, but a great deal of skill was involved in the production of the double-edged, straight blade. The surface was patterned with a series of lines running up the center, and these were produced during the complex hammering and twisting of the metal which formed the blade. Hard cutting edges were welded to the core, and the whole blade was then ground and polished. Most blades were about three feet long and two inches wide.

A smaller, dagger-like weapon was the *seax*, or *scramasax*, and this had a single-edged blade, the length of which varied considerably. Some swords and *seaxes* had words or symbols engraved on the blades, although this was not common practice until the ninth century. Spears were used both for throwing and thrusting, and the head varied with the purpose of the weapon — those that were thrown were small and light, whereas those for thrusting were large and sometimes barbed. Axes were also used as weapons.

Saxon shields, axes, and swords were often well decorated.

Vikings sometimes wore visored helmets such as the seventh-century example on the right and fought with swords and axes. But one of their most important possessions was the long ship, along whose sides the rowers hung their shields to form a protective wall. In these broad, shallow craft crews of raiders crossed great seas and reached lands as far apart as Britain and Russia.

Vikings

In their longships the Vikings took trade and terror to almost every country in Europe and many in Africa and Asia; they even reached America. At first their ships kept near the coast, but soon their skill and courage enabled them to venture across miles of open sea. They came from Sweden, Norway, and Denmark, and their first recorded attack on Britain was in A.D. 787, when the crews of three ships sacked the town of Poole. They left, but later they were to return in large numbers.

A great host of Danish raiders roamed Britain, plundering and killing, until they were defeated by Alfred the Great in 878. The Danes fought on foot with weapons very similar to those of the Saxons. Shields were still round and made of leather-covered wood, reinforced with metal. On the back was one strap through which the user passed his hand to grasp a bar at the center. A hole was cut at the center of the shield to accommodate the clenched hand; to guard the hand, a raised dome, the shield boss, was secured over the hole. Most of these bosses were quite plain, but some like that from the Sutton Hoo ship were very elaborate.

27

Viking equipment

Many of the Viking warriors relied solely on their shields for defense, but their leaders, no doubt, wore a byrnie (a coat of mail). These byrnies had short sleeves and usually reached only to the waist, although some were long enough to reach to the knees. A few may have been strengthened by the addition of metal plates, but it is not clear exactly how these were made. Helmets were not uncommon, and many were surmounted by a figure of a boar. Many helmets were conical with a wide brim, and it seems that often some kind of badge was painted on the front to assist recognition. Despite a romantic belief that all Viking helmets were decorated with wings or horns, there is only scanty evidence that such helmets were ever used.

Viking swords were cleverly designed for easy use in action, and this was achieved by tapering the blade toward the point —it meant that there was less weight at the point, so permitting freer movement. This type of blade was common to the majority of Viking swords, but the style of hilt varied considerably, and as many as nine have been identified. Most have a simple cross-guard, either straight or slightly drooping, and it was in the pommel that there were so many variations.

Popular with Vikings, and later with Normans, was the simple, conical helmet with a straight nasal to guard the face.

The straight-bladed Viking sword was for slashing; a single-edged *seax* (*bottom*) was also popular.

Viking axes

Although the Vikings were expert swordsmen, they did not eschew other weapons such as spears and axes. The spears of the Saxons and Vikings, used both for thrusting and throwing, had a shaft of ash about seven feet long. One end was tipped with iron, and the leaf-shaped head fitted on the other by means of a long socket which had two side bars. Since the spear was a favorite hunting weapon, these bars served to prevent too deep a penetration into wild boar and other prey.

Even more deadly was the great, two-handed Danish axe; the wedge-shaped head with its curved edge was fitted to the end of a six-foot haft. Swung in great arcs, they could cut through shield and armor. This Danish axe was a favorite weapon of the housecarls, an élite group of paid warriors, both Viking and Saxon, who guarded their king and constituted the core of the Saxon army at Hastings. In battle they formed a line with shields touching edge to edge to create a defensive wall.

ELEVENTH CENTURY

Normans

Some of the Danish sea rovers sailed up the Seine and captured the town of Rouen, making it their headquarters and settling in the surrounding countryside. Charles, the ruler of France, recognized that they could not be evicted and made a treaty with them, ceding the area to these Northmen, Normans, in return for their allegiance to him. The contract was sealed by the marriage of the King's daughter Ghisela and the Danish leader Rollo who, according to one account, agreed to the marriage on hearing that she was of suitable height. Rollo was acclaimed Duke of Normandy, his descendants extended their hold on the north of France, and their lands became known as Normandy. It was from this stock that William, Duke of Normandy, sprang, being confirmed in his title at the age of seven when his father Robert made a pilgrimage to Jerusalem.

On the Bayeux Tapestry, Norman archers are shown using short bows, and accounts of the Battle of Hastings stress their great use of this weapon. Some archers are shown wearing mail hauberks (*left*), while others lack any armor. During the latter part of the eleventh century there was a gradual increase in the use of the crossbow (*below*).

Cavalry formed the main arm of the Norman forces, and the knights, clad in mail from head to knee, fought with lance, sword, and club and guarded themselves with long, kite-shaped shields.

Mailed knights

The Vikings, after landing from their ships, had frequently rounded up all the available horses and turned themselves into mounted infantry. The Normans developed this into a real cavalry and when William, Duke of Normandy, landed in England in October 1066, the most important section of his army was composed of mailed cavalry. These knights, mounted on small horses, were covered from head to knee with mail, and their heads were also protected by conical helmets fitted with single-bar nasals. For extra protection they carried a kite-shaped shield, and this was sufficiently large to cover the rider from neck to toe.

In battle these knights fought with sword, mace, and lance. Their legs were usually left unprotected, but on their feet they wore simple, pointed prick-spurs. Similarly armed Normans fought Arab and Byzantine in Sicily and southern Italy. The expense of arms and armor helped to bring about the division between knight or noble and the rest of the population of Europe.

The Crusades

In A.D. 1095 Pope Urban sent out the call for the rescue of Jerusalem from the followers of Mohamed. The resulting Crusades were to force Western Europe and the Near East into close contact for the next 300 years. The differences between the various peoples of Europe were broken down when Norman, Dane, German, French and Italian knights were comrades on the same battlefield and knightly weapons became standardized all over Europe.

From Arab swordsmiths Europeans learned how to forge better steel, as the famous Damascus and Toledo blades showed, though the shape of the sword remained reasonably constant. From Byzantine engineers Europeans learned about building great stone castles with rounded flanking towers. Those, in turn, meant an emphasis on siege engines, though even then castles could usually be taken only by long sieges or treachery.

The Crusaders found that their heavy armor would enable Western knights to smash through more numerous but more lightly armed foes, though care had to be taken that the horses would not be worn out. As a result armor tended to become heavier, and eventually plate replaced chain armor.

The Krak of the Chevaliers. This crusader castle served to guard Palestine's northern approaches.

A crusader armed in the manner
typical for the 1st and 2nd crusade.

Returning Crusaders brought their new found knowledge
back with them and soon stone castles sprouted on many a
European hill. Also back came silken surcoats to go over
armor and slim daggers to slip through links of steel. The
curved saber, the scimitar, was known but scorned as an
infidel weapon because of its resemblance to the Islamic
crescent.

TWELFTH CENTURY

Swords

There was little real difference between the sword of the Norman warrior and that of his ancestors, the Danes or Vikings. All used their swords primarily as slashing weapons, although the Normans increasingly used the point in combat. The blade was fairly long and tapered slightly to the point, and its weight was reduced by the cutting of a shallow groove centrally along its length. This groove, known as the fuller, is often erroneously described as a blood gutter. Some of the earlier blades bore a maker's name inset in large letters.

Protection for the hand was afforded by a cross-guard at the top of the blade; it had arms, quillons, normally straight but occasionally slightly down-curving. From the center top of the blade projected a narrow extension called the tang, and around this were secured two strips of wood, tightly bound in position by cord or leather thonging. To balance the weight of the blade and ensure easy handling, a weight, the pommel, was secured at the end of the tang. Pommels varied considerably and offer useful evidence in dating swords. Many of them were simply a semi-circular block fitted to a T-bar at the end of the tang. Norman swords tended to have longer, straighter guards than the earlier examples, and the pommel was less like a recumbent D and more like a brazil-nut in shape. All available evidence suggests that the Norman swords were designed for use in one hand and that the hilts offering room for a two-handed grip were a later development.

When not in use, the sword was housed in a scabbard which hung at the side, normally the left, secured by a belt and straps. Some illustrations show the scabbard worn under the mail, in which case the hilt projected through a slit in the side. Scabbards were made from two strips of wood covered with leather and strengthened at the mouth by a metal guard, and at the tip was a more elaborate guard known as the chape.

Many examples of these swords have survived, and such weapons figure prominently in the battle scenes on the Bayeux Tapestry, although the majority of horsemen are shown wielding spears. Swords were to change little until the 1500's when hilts and blades became more elaborate.

Normans used, among others, the Viking sword with its straight
cutting blade and quillons. Pommels were more varied in shape.

35

Bayeux devices

The Norman kite shield was fitted on the inside with short straps for holding and a longer one which could be used to sling the shield over the back when not in use. All the mounted Normans depicted on the Bayeux Tapestry are shown with this typical, long, kite-shaped shield, and each shield bears some form of decoration. In some cases it is no more than a band of color around the edge; in others it is a series of dots which may represent nails or rivets, or may be purely decorative. Many show far more elaborate patterns; crosses are very common, and some bear dragons or other mythical creatures. Even if we accept the tapestry as true representation rather than artistic interpretation, it does not prove that the use of such patterns and pictures was anything other than decorative and haphazard. Heraldry is, above all, a regulated code, and heraldic arms are inherited; there is no evidence to suggest that the Normans observed either point. Shield faces were, of course, obvious places for displaying arms long after shields had been abandoned on the battlefield.

On many of the shields shown on the Bayeux Tapestry there are patterns and animal shapes, but they are not truly heraldic.

The lion *motif* on the shield and helmet of the figure on Richard I's great seal is one of the earlier examples of true heraldry.

Beginnings of heraldry

Increasing protection by armor and helmets raised certain problems, for it became difficult to distinguish friend from foe as the face was gradually more and more obscured. Eventually facial recognition became impossible, and it was necessary to establish identity by other means, hence the beginnings of heraldry. Earlier races such as the Greeks, Romans, and Normans had used symbols and effigies to aid identification, but their use seems to have been haphazard, and it is not until the twelfth century that anything like a formal system of heraldry appears.

One of the earliest examples of a recognizable coat-of-arms is that shown on the seals of Richard I (1189–99). Both seals feature lions on the shield. However, much more interesting is the placing of the lions on the crest worn on top of the helmet which, following contemporary fashion, completely covered the face. It may safely be assumed that the use of such badges had been well established for some time before Richard's reign, and here may be seen the beginnings of the complicated science of heraldry.

A broad band from top left to lower right is known as a bend.

Horizontally crossing the center of the shield is the fess.

Scottish heraldry favors the St. Andrew's cross, the saltire.

Heraldic shields

From the design point of view the long kite shield is awkward, and for heraldry its shape was altered to a more triangular form with greater width and less length—a shape often likened to the base of a pressing iron. More elaborate is the *ecusson à bouche,* which has a notch in the top corner, originally to accommodate the lance. There were other types of shield as well, and all were divided into nine sections in order that the description, blazoning, of arms could be accurate, although in English heraldry two of the sections were very seldom used.

One point of confusion in heraldry is undoubtedly that the sides of a shield are defined as if seen by the holder; hence the right hand (dexter in correct terminology) appears on the left when seen from the front. All the signs and devices used have their correct heraldic description; thus a broad band crossing the shield diagonally from the top left-hand corner, dexter chief, to the lower right, sinister base, is known as a bend. A broad band crossing the shield horizontally is defined as fess, and two diagonal bands producing a St. Andrew's cross are designated saltire. The conventional cross is officially a Greek cross and can be used with a number of variations in detail—over 300 are accepted by the heraldic authorities! There are also strict rules set down about the combining of charges.

Although the origins of heraldry were largely practical, it soon became a complicated and involved science. As time passed and families inter-married, the arms became more and more concerned with, and complicated by, distinctions for various members of the family. Despite the numerous variations produced it was still possible for two families to claim the use of identical, or similar, arms. To settle such disputes a special body of officials was created in the mid-fourteenth century, and today the College of Arms in London is the supreme authority on all matters heraldic in England. In countries with no royalty, heraldry is less closely controlled but there are geneological societies in almost all European countries and America.

A conventionally shaped cross is known as the Greek cross.

Division of the shield in this style is called wavy, or *ordée*.

This is the baton sinister, a symbol indicating illegitimacy.

Mail

Mail was a versatile form of body defense, although its construction was a long and tedious business. First, the metal was drawn out into wire, wrapped around a former, and cut into open-ended circles. In European mail, each link was then interwoven with adjoining links and the ends were flattened, drilled, and riveted together.

Mail coats, fitted with short sleeves and extending from neck to waist or knee, were highly prized by the Vikings, and sagas such as *Beowulf* make frequent reference to them. The coat of mail, usually referred to as the hauberk or byrnie, was carefully shaped in much the same way as a piece of knitting, with increases and decreases in the number of links. In the majority of cases the links were so arranged that each one was connected to four others. One great advantage of mail was its flexibility: it was supple enough to allow movement with little or no hindrance.

Beneath the mail, the knight wore some form of padded garment to afford extra protection and prevent the rings from chafing and catching on his skin or undergarments. Not only was the knight's body encased in mail, but a mail hood, the coif was used to give protection to the head. Later, mail sleeves were lengthened and the ends modified to form a pair of hand coverings known as mufflers. Legs were also protected by mail, either in the form of strips of mail tied on to cover the front of the legs or 'stockings' of mail which were probably held in place by straps.

Mail was not without its disadvantages, not the least being its weight, which pressed mainly upon the shoulders. With a strong blow from a sword or lance there was also a danger of

Mail was a main form of defense for many centuries and was made up of a series of interlocking rings of metal. Each link was usually arranged to join with four surrounding ones. The ends of the links were flattened, drilled, and then riveted together, the whole forming a flexible metal defense.

links splitting and being pushed into the skin, resulting in a possibly mortal septic wound. The only easy way of strengthening the mail was to use thicker rings, but this rendered the mail less flexible. However, despite these significant drawbacks, mail was to remain a common form of defense until the late seventeenth century.

Mail and scale defenses were often combined and during the eleventh and twelfth centuries extended to cover most of the body.

Helmets

Norman helmets were delightfully functional, lacking all un-necessary 'frills' and designed to afford maximum protection. There were two varieties of simple, conical helmet worn over the coif—one hammered from a single piece of metal and perhaps reinforced with a band around the brim, and the other fashioned from a number of sections, with joints reinforced and covered by metal ribs. A nasal, a bar projecting down from the brim, gave some protection from a slash to the face. According to contemporary accounts, William had to raise his helmet during the Battle of Hastings to show that he was still alive, indicating that the nasal was probably large enough to obscure most of the face. A similar bar was sometimes fitted at the back of the helmet to guard the neck.

During the twelfth century some helmets had earflaps fitted, and the neck-guard was made larger. Toward the end of the century a number of styles were in use, including some helmets with a rounded or flat top. Both must have been unsatisfactory for, unlike the conical type, there was no glancing surface to deflect a blow.

Facial protection had been increased at the end of the eleventh century when a face-guard, cut with slots for sight

Instead of the conical Norman helmet the twelfth-century knight sometimes wore a flat-topped helmet with a nasal (*below*). The face-protecting plates increased in size until they joined the neck-guard to form a tubular helmet (*right*).

The helmet at the top, known as a kettle hat, was worn by troops over many centuries. The helm, which completely covered the head, was made in a variety of styles, one is shown on the right, but many still preferred the conical type with a nasal.

and numerous holes for ventilation, was added to the helmet. Here was the beginning of the later helmets which completely covered the head. Another type of helmet was the kettle hat, which derived its name from its fancied resemblance to an upturned cauldron. This type was much simpler than the others and as such was favored by many, remaining in use, with minor changes in style, for centuries. All these helmets were tied onto the head with laces.

THIRTEENTH CENTURY
Swords

Although the axe, now fitted on shafts about four feet long, was still a popular weapon, the sword held pride of place. It was carried by both cavalry and infantry and, at the beginning of the thirteenth century, had altered but little from that used at Hastings. Blades were slightly longer and had a more pronounced tip, suggesting a greater use of the point. Fullers were usually narrower, an increasing tendency as the centuries passed. Quillons were still most often straight, but some were curved slightly downward. Pommels were still mostly of the D- or brazil-nut shape, but there was an increasing use of circular pommels, and during the last 20 years of the twelfth century many had had their edges beveled. A number of swords of this period have been discovered, and many of them have the inlaid inscriptions found on earlier swords.

Swords changed little in the twelfth and thirteenth centuries.

The sword continued to develop as the improvement in armor forced the swordsmith to seek more efficient means of breaking through the knight's defenses. To increase the cutting force of a blow the blades were lengthened, and the hilts were made long enough for them to be gripped by both hands. Pommels were now more likely to be wheel-shaped, but many variations were used. Another way of breaching the defenses was to use a stabbing sword to pierce the links of mail or slip under the unprotected joints of armor, and such weapons had stiff, narrow blades. A third solution offered by the sword-smith was the falchion, which was a shorter sword with a curved, single-edged blade widening toward the tip, thus ensuring that most weight was at the point where the sword edge was most likely to strike home. Daggers were carried by knights, but they were only used as a last resort or to kill a downed opponent.

One new variety was the wide-bladed falchion (*second from left*).

Plate armor

Scale armor was a very old form of defense, and during the thirteenth century long coats of it were sometimes used, although mail was the form of protection worn by most knights. There is evidence that armorers were producing garments, much like tunics, which were reinforced with plates of metal, and that these were worn over the mail. This coat of plates appeared during the early part of the thirteenth century and continued in use during most of the fourteenth century as well.

Riders' legs were especially vulnerable, and it is not surprising that there were attempts to reinforce their defenses. Thighs were fitted with padded covers, and around the middle of the thirteenth century small plates were used to cover the knees. Called poleyns, these plates were fitted to the mail chausses or to the quilted thigh-pieces and although quite small at first were soon big enough to encircle the knee. Metal plates were also made to guard the shins.

Armor for the arms followed a similar pattern, and small, circular plates, couters, were fitted at the elbows from about

All three soldiers wear mail as the prime defense. They also wear (*left to right*) scale armor, a gambeson, and a coat of plates.

Great helms became more massive and were often reinforced around the eye slits and at the junction of plates (*see page 48*).

1260. It is possible that gutter-like plates were used on the arms, but there is no evidence of this until much later. Protection for the hand, in the form of gauntlets, was also being improved, and such materials as whalebone, brass, and *cuir-bouilli* (leather hardened by treatment with hot wax) were all employed. By the end of the thirteenth century, gauntlets entirely of metal plates were certainly in use.

At the end of the thirteenth century there appeared a plate defense for the neck, a gorget, which extended up as far as the nose and down over the shoulders. Most of the plate armor of the thirteenth century was worn only by mounted knights. The infantry wore much simpler protective devices such as the hauberk with long sleeves and a coif. Some wore shorter coats of mail which were known as haubergeons, but many had only a padded tunic, a gambeson, and possibly a simple helmet such as a kettle hat.

Knights

Knights of the thirteenth century were guarded from head to foot by a collection of protective garments including padding, mail, and plate. Upon his head the knight wore a tight-fitting, padded cap covered with a metal coif which was fitted with a strip of mail, the aventail, to cover the chin. Over this went the helmet, which could be a kettle hat or a round-topped helmet with a nasal. For greater protection the knight wore a great helm which, being cylindrical, completely encircled the head. It was flat topped and had slits for sights, the edges of which were reinforced with bars; to facilitate breathing, small holes were drilled in the lower front section. The body was encased in layers of padded garments and mail, with the possible addition of plate at elbows, knees, and throat, and on the gauntlets. Over all this went the long tunic known as the surcoat, which may also have been reinforced with plates. Some knights also wore over the hauberk a body defense known as the cuirie, made of *cuir-bouilli.*

From about 1250, horses were protected by two curtains of mail reaching halfway down the legs and covering the neck and head. Such loose mail must have been heavy and restrictive. Since both rider and horse were now well covered it was imperative that some form of recognition be worn, and the use of heraldic devices further increased, with crests painted on helmets and other flat surfaces, including small plates, ailettes, attached to the shoulders. These were of treated leather, whalebone, and metal and were worn at the end of the thirteenth and beginning of the fourteenth centuries. From a belt hung the scabbard, the fitting of which was so designed as to make the sword hang at an angle.

Sword-belts were elaborately laced to ensure that the sword hung at a comfortable angle.

There was an increasing use of extra reinforcing plates at knees, elbows, and the throat, although mail still predominated. The head was protected by a coif which often covered a metal skull-cap and over all went a kettle hat or great helm. Heraldry was well established, and arms were displayed on shields, ailettes, and surcoats.

49

FOURTEENTH CENTURY

Swords

At the end of the thirteenth century swords had already begun to develop into specialized forms, unlike the earlier stabbing weapons. They were also becoming less the weapon of the nobility. Many were longer and heavier, to increase the force now required to make any impression on the greatly improved body defenses of the knights. Grips tended to be longer, affording room for the two-handed swing with its greater force. Swords with long, stiff, narrow blades were produced, and these were intended to pierce the mail by concentrating the thrust on a small area. It was fashionable to secure a chain from the sword-hilt to the belt or, later, to a staple on the cuirie. Daggers and helmets were similarly protected against loss. Daggers with fairly short, tapering blades were only the last resort in combat and were usually carried on the right-hand side of the belt. Shields were much smaller, and foot soldiers usually carried a buckler.

Greater variety was now common in the details of swords.

Developments begun earlier continued during the fourteenth century, and specialized swords became the order of the day; indeed some knights carried two swords. At the belt, hung a general-purpose sword with a blade designed for stabbing and slashing and fitted with a straight, or slightly down-curving, cross-guard and a pommel which was wheel- or pear-shaped. Blades tended to be longer than previously, and to compensate for the extra weight pommels were somewhat larger. Blades tapered gradually to the point and were double-edged. Suspended from the saddle was the thrusting sword, with a stiff, narrow blade tapering acutely to the point, which might well be thickened for greater strength. There is evidence that this type of sword was used as a lance, the knight charging with the pommel against his shoulder. In order to obtain a more secure grip on these larger swords the first finger was looped over the cross-guard, and an inch or so of the blade was left blunt; this portion was called the ricasso.

Many swords were made longer, stiffer and used for thrusting.

Other weapons

Along with the sword, fourteenth-century European warriors had a considerable armory at their disposal, ranging from daggers to longbows. Axes, so popular with the Danes, remained a favorite weapon both with the foot soldier and the knight, who fought on horseback and on foot. For the horseman the axe-head was mounted on a short staff and often had a sharp spike on the back of the blade. For foot combat it was more common for the head to be mounted at the end of a long shaft, and in order to provide extra strength for the handle, long metal arms, langets, extended from the head along its sides. The edge of the axe-head was usually curved in order to give as much leverage and cutting power as possible. Like the shorter axes, they were fitted with a spike on the head. Clubs, simple, highly lethal, and ever-popular, continued in use. Maces, a type of club, were developing into a form which became common in the fifteenth century. Their heads were composed of a number of flanges arranged around the shaft.

For many of the foot soldiers called from their homes to serve in the feudal levy, their only weapons were those that they took with them, and in many instances these were domestic implements such as pitchforks, flails, or blades mounted on shafts for hedging. Some of the hedging tools were developed into a recognizable weapon, the bill, with a long cutting head and a small, rearward-pointing spike. Lances were used by mounted troops, and a shortened version, some five feet long, was used for foot combat. The 18-ft. Swiss pike was developed for use against mounted knights.

It was during the fourteenth century that the English archers first achieved their control of the battlefield. A thick shaft of yew, elm, or ash standing some six feet high and a stout linen string constituted the formidable longbow. The arrows, about three feet long, were of birch and were fitted with goose feathers and a variety of points. Each archer carried a bundle of about two dozen arrows pushed under his belt. With a pull of anything up to 100 pounds, the longbow demanded constant practice to master its use, but it was deadly up to a maximum range of 400 yards. Crossbows required far less skill and were very powerful, but they were much slower than longbows, which could discharge twelve arrows in the time it took to shoot one crossbow bolt.

Axes and maces (*above and below*) were still commonly used, although the latter now had flanged heads.

Longbows were gaining control on the battlefield, but crossbows were also more powerful and needed mechanical spanning aids: See the windlass (*below*). Bills were still common.

Helmets

The fourteenth century was a period of change, and a number of new types of helmet appeared. Great helms probably varied least of all, but their use was gradually restricted to the tournament instead of war. Some were made with loops at their base which were used to strap the helm in position.

The round-topped helmet of the thirteenth century was improved by making the crown more pointed. A blow from a weapon was now deflected and made to glance off, so that its force was dissipated. This type of helmet, the bascinet, was extended to cover the back of the neck and the sides of the head. At first the bascinet was worn over the coif, but after about 1320 the coif was abandoned and a short mail curtain, the aventail, was fitted to the rim of the helmet. Some bascinets were decorated with a circlet, like a small crown. Kettle hats were still worn by many mounted and foot troops and, although detail varied, most had a conical crown and a wide brim.

Bascinets became popular, and the great helm (*bottom*) tended to be restricted to tilting.

During the fourteenth century the moveable face-piece, the visor, appeared, enabling the wearer to bare his face when there was no danger. Some visors were pivoted at the sides of the helmet, whereas others were hinged at the brow. Visors were flat at first, but gradually they became rounded. The sights were no longer mere slits but had surrounding flanges for extra protection. Ventilation holes (it must have been extremely stuffy inside the helmet) were numerous, although sometimes only drilled on the right side of the visor. Some visors were rounded, whereas others had a snouted appearance; helmets with the latter were often called pig-faced bascinets. Bascinet visors were made detachable; like hinges, they were fitted with securing pins which could be withdrawn to release the visor. Bascinets were either worn beneath a great helm without the visor or on their own either with or without the visor. The aventail extended over the shoulders and was secured to the rim of the bascinet by staples and laces.

Face visors were attached to bascinets at the brow or side and could be raised or lowered.

Armor

Plate armor became far more common during the fourteenth century and was extended to all parts of the body. Curved plates were secured to the outside of legs and arms, and the plates at elbow and knee were lengthened to overlap them; eventually all were secured by hinges to form a complete arm or leg defense. Gauntlets, at first of mail, were strengthened by metal plates, the fingers being fitted with individual, small plates which allowed free movement.

Body armor was also being developed, and the most common form was that of metal hoops riveted to a leather garment. There is some evidence to suggest that a small, solid breast-plate was worn by some knights. Hauberks often had a stiffened collar which stood up to protect the neck. Inventories of this period occasionally mention a form of collar called a pizaine, but its exact nature is uncertain. It was possibly a separate collar of stiffened mail. Rigidity was given by the

Dating from about 1370, this brass of Ralph de Knevynton from Essex shows a skirt of hoops fastened to fabric.

use of thick links. Mail was still the prime defense, but it was reinforced by a padded tunic, the aketon, worn beneath it and a coat of plates over it. Over all went the surcoat, now shortened at the front, and the extra plate defenses.

Plate armor
Arm-pieces now comprised two plates which completely circled the upper part of the arm, and the shoulder was guarded by a number of shaped metal strips called lames. Similarly, the shin was enclosed within two plates, while at the knee the poleyn was fitted with a shaped extension to afford some protection to the back of the joint. Later in the century the thigh was also given plate defenses. Metal plates, resembling civilian shoes in shape, guarded the feet.

By 1360 many breast-plates were probably composed of a single plate, whereas the skirt defense was still fashioned out of a number of metal hoops. In some cases the back-plates were dispensed with, and the breast-plate and front skirt were simply secured over the mail with straps crossing at the back. Some of the illustrations of the period also show straps to hold down the aventail of the bascinet. Guard chains were still used occasionally to secure the sword and dagger to the breast-plate as a precaution against loss.

In the fourteenth century mittens of plate (*left*) replaced those of mail. Plate gauntlets appeared (*right*) and from 1375 onward were quite common. Design improved until one large plate guarded the back of the hand and smaller ones the fingers (*center*).

Knights

Armor during the fourteenth century was extremely diverse. As time passed there was a continuing and increasing emphasis on the use of plate armor, but many styles were worn and it must not be assumed that any single fashion was universal. Many knights saw little military service and were content to retain their old-fashioned armor, while others, with greater need and more money (for armor was expensive), discarded older pieces and purchased the latest styles. Even with new styles a number of variations could be found; for instance, some knights fought wearing visors, while others preferred greater freedom and accepted the greater risk by discarding the visor completely. A variety of helmets was available, and any type might be worn with the armor, including the great helm and the simple kettle hat.

Heraldry was now well established and well-developed, and its effects were to

Mail, plate, a padded aketon, and a coat of plates make up the defenses worn by Sir John de Creke (c. 1325); by this date many knights were carrying a much smaller shield.

be seen in many walks of life. Early in the fourteenth century the ailettes were discarded, but the practice of carrying banners was still observed by many knights. Some knights adopted a tight-fitting tunic on which was embroidered their coat-of-arms, and some had the tunic padded as well, so that it afforded a little extra protection. There was an increase in decorative fashions, and an elaborate, jeweled belt began to be worn fastened across the hips. Toward the end of the century the sword and dagger were attached to this belt, probably with small hooks.

Some of the nobles had their armor decorated with engravings or edgings of gold, silver, and brass. There are numerous contemporary references to decorations of velvet and precious stones, but few examples, if any, have survived. Most of the evidence for the study of armor of this period is drawn from brasses, effigies, and manuscripts; actual examples are extremely rare.

Arm defenses were fairly well developed by about 1325, as shown on this brass of Sir William Fitzralph from Essex. Mail still predominates, but plate is becoming more popular.

FIFTEENTH CENTURY

Helmets

In Italy a style of helmet closely resembling the ancient Greek Corinthian appeared, although it seems to have been abandoned by about 1470. Known as the *barbuta,* it had a smooth skull, which was extended to the shoulders, and at the front was a T-shaped opening for the nose and eyes. A similar *barbuta* had a simpler, wider facial opening; this form survived until the end of the century.

Another, far more complex helmet which apparently originated in Italy was the armet *(see page 62).* For the tournament, knights still favored a version of the great helm; as the lower lip of the sight projected forward it gained the name of frog-mouthed helmet. The projecting lower lip was designed in such a way that when the knight was seated upright it was so positioned as to prevent any blade from entering.

Although the kettle helmet seems to have fallen out of fa-

Bascinets dating from the early part of the fifteenth century which show some of the many possible variations of this type.

vor in Italy during the fifteenth century, this certainly was not the case in Germany, where it was as popular as ever. Many had small crowns and deeply down-drooping brims from which a section had been cut to allow the wearer to see. With the kettle hat the knight often wore a bevor, a shaped plate guarding the lower face, the neck, and the top of the chest.

Sallets were also popular in Germany and were often distinguished by a long, laminated, pointed tail to guard the neck. At the front, half or full visors were fitted. Late in the fifteenth century there appeared a German sallet which had a very short tail and a closer-fitting skull; a flat visor, pierced with slits, completed the helmet. Great bascinets were common in Germany; these had the aventail replaced by solid plates and were normally fitted with a hinged visor. The large, rounded helmet was fastened to the body armor by straps which held it rigid, not moving with the head.

The hinged visors fitted to bascinets were extremely varied in shape, but all had numerous, very necessary ventilation holes.

Armets

Bascinets were long to serve the knight, but armorers of the fifteenth century were, no doubt, seeking newer and more convenient types of helmet. One style, the armet, probably originated in Italy and was to be adopted and modified all over Europe. It was first illustrated early in the century in Bavaria on a German effigy of a knight who died in 1416, and by the middle of the century it was not uncommon. Basically it consisted of a skull, usually rounded, very rarely pointed, which was extended to about ear level. From the back a strip of metal extended downward as far as the neck, following the shape of the head. Two shaped cheek-pieces, hinged at the top to the skull, could be closed to cover the entire face. These side plates slightly overlapped the 'tail' at the back and were locked at the front by a catch. A gap of an inch or so allowed the wearer to see; on a few armets this space was left unprotected, but on most there was a small visor, pivoted at the sides, which reduced the open gap to a minimum at which clear vision and safety were compatible; many visors could be detached from the

1

3

5

62

2

4

Helmets from Italy and Germany show how the pieces of an armet fit together. Hinged to the skull were two cheek-pieces (1). Pivoted at the side was a visor and secured to the crown was a strengthening plate (2-4). A wrapper, sometimes lengthened by gorget plates, was strapped on below the visor (5). Origin of the examples: 1. Italian (c. 1430); 2. Milanese (c. 1440); 3. Italian (c. 1475); 4. Italian (c. 1550); 5. Innsbruck (c. 1505).

helmet simply by removing the hinge pins.

Extra protection for the face was obtained by a shaped piece of armor, the wrapper, which was strapped on to cover the front of the helmet below the visor. A strap encircling the neck was protected at the back by a large, decorative rondel fitted at the bottom of the tail. At the top of the wrapper there was a small slot which accommodated a bar projecting from the side of the visor; this served as a convenient handle for raising and lowering the visor. Some wrappers were lengthened by the addition of a few gorget plates which extended down to protect the chest. Greater strength for the brow of the helmet was obtained by a shaped plate permanently secured to the skull, and around 1460 the top of the plate was ridged slightly, again to give extra strength.

As the century went on, the face opening became progressively larger—a trend which reached its peak with the close helmets. German armets produced early in the sixteenth century had wider tails and cheek-pieces hinged, not at the top, but at the back of the side plates.

Knights

During the early fifteenth century two distinct styles of armor were developed—one originating in Italy and the other in Germany. Both styles had certain peculiarities, but each influenced the other and they were often combined.

The Italian armor, produced at Milan and Pisa, tended to have smooth, rounded outlines with large shoulder defenses, pauldrons, curving over to give a 'chunky' appearance. Extra plates were often added to the shoulder defenses, and the poleyns at the knees and the couters at the elbows were curved around to afford maximum protection. Breast-plates were of two overlapping plates, allowing the wearer some flexibility of movement. Since the lance was held under the right arm, the plates on the right side of the armor were specially shaped to take it. From about 1380 a lance-rest was a common feature; this was a bracket fitted on the right side of the breast-plate, and it was intended to take the shock of the blow when the lance struck its target. On the fifteenth-century Italian armors this lance-rest was detachable, secured by a pin and a series of bars. From the lower edge of the breast-plate hung a series of hoops forming the fauld, and from the bottom of these hung another plate, the tasset. Other refinements included the raised rib placed at the tip of the thigh-pieces and at the edge of the breast-plate, around the neck and armholes. This served to deflect the point of a weapon sliding over the surface of the armor.

Outside Germany the Italian style was now generally used, although there were variations in detail. The armors of English knights during the early part of the fifteenth century had an almost smooth outline with a breast- and back-plate hinged on the left and secured on the right by straps. A skirt of hoops hung around the waist, the arms were completely enclosed in plates, and the hands were encased in plate gauntlets. To guard the armpits, always vulnerable and yet difficult to protect, small metal discs were attached to the shoulders. Mail was also used for protection, and beneath his armor the knight wore an arming doublet, a padded garment with patches of mail stitched on at vulnerable points. In donning his armor the knight worked from the feet upward, leaving the gauntlets and helmet for last.

Italian armors showing the change from the late fourteenth (*left top and bottom*) to the mid-fifteenth century (*right*).

The German style of armor was one of the most attractive ever produced. It first began to develop around 1460 and continued to be popular until the end of the fifteenth century, although it underwent minor modifications. This armor, known as Gothic, was produced in Nuremberg, Augsburg, and Innsbruck among others. The style is characterized by an elongated, slender outline and a decoration of points and fluting. The fluting served the double purpose of giving extra strength to the plates and helping to deflect weapon points from vital areas. Many of the pieces were wedged with brass. The helmet most often worn was the sallet, and a throat-guard, the bevor, was worn as well.

The breast-plate was like its Italian counterpart, usually of two plates, whereas the top of the shoulder was protected by a series of curved metal plates, spaulders, and the armpit by a besagew. Some armorers tended to exaggerate the style, and some armors had grotesque couters with enormous spikes. Gauntlets had long, pointed cuffs, bearing the typical, graceful fluting and scalloped edges.

Gothic armor of the late fifteenth century with fine form and graceful outline. (*Opposite*) helmets were the sallet type (*see page 61*), some with laminated neck-pieces (*top*). Gauntlets had long, pointed cuffs and the characteristic curved ridging; both fingered and mitten types were made.

(*Left*) one of the finest of Gothic armors was made at Augsburg (*c.* 1480) and belonged to the Archduke Sigmund of Tyrol. (*Above*) a later, simpler form of Gothic armor.

A pivoted arm on the quintain administered a sharp blow to a careless rider—a speedy method of instruction for young squires!

Tournaments

It was not easy for a knight encumbered with mail or other armor to manage a spirited horse and wield a long lance or a sword at the same time; in fact it required practice and training. For those of sufficient standing to be eligible for knighthood, riding was second nature acquired in childhood. Skill at arms had, however, to be learned. Serving as a squire to a knight taught a youngster the theory of knighthood, but practical experience had to be gained the hard way.

The quintain was a simple but effective device to practice on and was made up of a pivoted arm set on top of a pole. At one end of the arm was some form of target, perhaps in the shape of a Turk's head, and at the opposite end a weight was suspended. Charging at the quintain, the rider struck the target with his lance and then had to follow through, avoiding the weight as it swung around; lack of skill meant a hefty clout and a good chance of being unhorsed.

When some degree of competence had been achieved, it was time to turn to more active methods and here the *mêlée,* or tournament, played an important part, for this was, in effect, a practice war. Large groups of knights took part in these mock battles which could, and did, cover many miles of countryside. On more 'formal' occasions the combat took place in a limited space. Tournaments became great social occasions, with knights traveling long distances to participate. Some monarchs viewed them with suspicion as places where rebellion could be plotted and for this reason forbad them unless special permission had been granted. Ordinary or blunted weapons were used in these contests, and for the winners there were opportunities to gain handsome prizes given by the organizer, in addition to the right to claim the armor and horse of the vanquished. Great sums of money were expended on these spectacles, and surviving accounts show that often special crests and weapons were purchased.

The tilt which was run with the riders on opposite sides of a wooden barrier so ensuring greater safety (*see page 71*).

Tilting armor

One of the popular pastimes of the nobility during the Middle Ages was that of tilting. In the early days the emphasis had been on mass combat, with groups of knights staging mock battles in the tourney. Many tournaments started as friendly combats but, as tempers frayed and blows became harder, they changed into small-scale wars with killed and wounded on both sides. This mass combat was gradually replaced by single combat or jousts. Sometimes the weapons were blunted, but often they were the same as those used in war. Since most knights had no desire to lose their lives unnecessarily, heavy armor was developed especially for the joust early in the fourteenth century. Extra pieces of armor were strapped into place, and the vamplate, a hand-guard, was fixed onto the

Special forms of armor were designed for the tilt and tournament. (*Below left and opposite right*) German armors for the *Gestech*. (*Below right*) a foot combat armor from Italy (*c.* 1490). (*Opposite left*) an Austrian armor for the *Scharfrennen*.

lance. Shields were also strapped on, and the lance was couched across the horse's neck so that riders charged each other shield to shield.

About 1420 a new style of tilting was introduced; a wooden fence separated the opponents and so reduced the chances of horses colliding. Great helms were still popular for tilting, but in Europe more specialized types of armor were made for different styles of combat.

For *Scharfrennen* the (the running tilt with sharp lances), enormous, semi-circular vamplates gave protection to the entire right side of the body. The German *Gestech* was fought with blunted or rebated lances which were fitted with three- or four-pronged heads. In this type of combat the aim was either to splinter the lance or unhorse an opponent. Great helms were worn, and a small, wooden shield was laced onto the left side of the body. Since the tilt offered protection for the lower part of the body, it was usual to leave the legs free of armor.

Horse armor

Archaeological and sculptural evidence clearly shows that forms of horse armor were used by heavy cavalry in the later Roman period. Mail trappings, reaching almost to the horse's feet, were worn then, but later their use seems to have been abandoned until the middle of the twelfth century. Even then the only common form was apparently a head defense, the chanfron. Mail defenses were in use during the thirteenth century, and there are many references to padded horse armors at that time.

Coats of plate similar to those worn by men were also used. Larger plates of leather and metal were introduced late in the thirteenth century, and one of the first pieces was a peytral, worn on the horse's chest. In the early fourteenth century

Mail was one of the earliest forms of horse armor and was used by the Romans. Plate defenses were gradually developed, becoming most common during the fifteenth and sixteenth centuries. Nevertheless, horse armor was very nearly abandoned by the early seventeenth century.

there are references to plates fitted over the rest of the horse's body, flanchards at the side and cruppers at the rear. For the neck, a combined piece of mail and plate, known as the crinet, was used. By the fifteenth century the plates were generally larger and more extensive, and in many instances the horse's armor, the bard, was decorated in exactly the same style as that of the knight. During the sixteenth century bards were far more common, and full armors as well as lighter types using smaller chanfrons, often protecting only the top of the head, were popular. Horse armor was gradually discarded during the second half of the sixteenth century, and by the end of the first quarter of the seventeenth century it had largely been abandoned. The chanfron, or rather the half-chanfron, and the crinet were the last pieces to go.

Chanfron and crinet (*see pages 72–73*)

Saddles were sometimes of ivory, like this mid-fifteenth-century one from Germany; some were fitted with front plates *(above)* to protect the rider's legs. *(Left)* a chanfron.

Horse equipment

For the mounted knight, his horse was of prime importance and represented an expensive piece of equipment. Knights might well own at least three horses: a destrier, the prize steed; a courser for war; and a general riding horse or rounsey.

The saddle differed greatly from the modern riding model, for it was so designed that the rider almost stood in it. It was only with the evolution of the stirrup that a mounted warrior was able to make full use of his height, and this style of riding enabled him to use the sword or mace with the whole force of his body. Saddles were apparently first used by the Goths and probably copied from them by the Romans. The front, the pommel, of a Norman saddle was fairly low and curved forward, whereas the back, the cantle, was slightly taller but curved over in much the same way. As time passed, the cantle was heightened and the sides were curved around to enclose the back of the rider. The pommel was also extended and often faced with metal plates to protect the rider's legs. Wood, ivory, leather, and bone were all used in the construction of saddles, and their seats were padded with hay.

Spurs were at first very simple and had a single spike, the prick-spur, on a U-shaped arm which strapped around the foot, but about 1330 another type, with a spiked disc, the rowel, became more popular. At first the 'neck' of metal joining the rowel and U-shaped arm was very long, but it was gradually reduced, and in the seventeenth century it had a distinct, downward bend.

Stirrups first appeared in the eighth century A.D. and made a great difference to the rider, giving him greater purchase and control.

Swords and daggers

Although the basic weapon of this period was still the sword designed for slashing and thrusting, its hilt was beginning to acquire some of the loops and bars found on sixteenth- and seventeenth-century weapons. Blades varied in length and width, and it is difficult to generalize. Rigidity was obtained by the use of a central rib or by grinding down the edges to produce a flattened blade, triangular in section. Cross-guards were usually long and often curved toward the blade or, occasionally, into a horizontal S-shape.

Around the middle of the century there appeared an infantry sword on which one of the arms of the hilt curved up to the pommel, thus forming a hand-guard, the knuckle-bow. Pommels were of many types; many were wheel-shaped but equally common were those of pear or kite-like form. The practice of hooking a finger over the cross-guard to improve the grip was increasing, and apart from the blunt ricasso there were often down-curving loops on the quillons to protect the first finger. Sword-belts were fairly narrow and were worn at an angle across the hips. The daggers used by the knights at this time were mostly straight, stiff-bladed weapons with the hilt protected by a disc at either end of the grip; they were called rondel daggers.

(*Opposite*) during the fifteenth century the sword hilt began to acquire extra loops and guards and became generally more complex. However, the sword was still basically a cut-and-thrust weapon.

(*Above*) the extremely popular quillon dagger (*see pages 112–113*). (*Below*) the earlier rondel dagger was more of a military weapon.

Pole-arms and other weapons

During the fifteenth century there was a revival of the pike, especially by the Swiss, who wreaked havoc on their opponents when they first introduced new formations using this very long spear. Switzerland was, at this time, a source of hired troops, and many kings numbered Swiss mercenaries among their armies. For the purpose of repelling cavalry charges, the pike was ideal, for it had a shaft of ash up to 18 feet in length and a long, strengthened steel head. With the ranks carefully staggered, it was possible to present a solid hedge of steel points sufficient to deter any horseman.

The success of the Swiss tactics using the pike encouraged many other commanders to copy the system, and the pike remained a popular weapon until the invention of the bayonet. Lances were made so that they were thickest near the grip and tapered away in either direction. A vamplate was fitted around the shaft just in front of the grip. For light cavalry a simpler, straight shaft was more common.

Chivalry had begun to lose its pride of place during this

Two early sixteenth-century halberds and a corseque (*right*)

century, and the foot soldier was already coming to play a more important part in the art of warfare. In order to pierce the strong armor so commonly worn, it was necessary to concentrate the force of a hard blow on a small area. A variety of axes and pole-arms were produced, and most had some form of spike which could pierce an armor.

Pole-axes, also known as ravens' bills, were popular and effective, with spikes at both ends of the shaft for thrusting, a hammer-head, and an axe-head. Simpler but not dissimilar was the halberd, which had a spike and an axe-head as well as a spike at the tip. Most staff weapons had long side bars, langets, extending from the head along the shaft, for this gave additional strength to the shaft and also lessened the chances of the head being struck off.

The glaive, a cutting and stabbing weapon which resembled a scythe blade mounted on a shaft about five feet long, was also used

Pole-axes and halberds could be used as axes or spears. All feature langets, and one (*far left*) a rondel hand-guard.

by many foot soldiers because it was such a simple weapon. Bills were still used by many, again because they were simple and ready to hand for the peasant called to serve in the feudal levy.

Longbows continued to be weapons of importance throughout the century, and such victories as Agincourt in 1415, when English bowmen slaughtered thousands of French knights, made them feared by all. The archer guarded his wrist against the slap of the bowstring by a leather or horn bracer inside the left wrist.

Arrow-heads were made in a variety of designs, but war arrows had narrow points intended to punch through plate armor. Crossbows were made even more powerful by the use of composition and steel bows, but their use was still limited by their slow rate of discharge. However, one new feature which was beginning to play a more and more important part in battle was, of course, gunpowder; its use was spreading and armies were beginning to deploy groups of gunners.

Horsemen made use of their spears and lances, but in addition they had such devices as the war hammer and mace. War hammers were, in effect, miniature pole-axes. A shaft of metal or wood, the wood being strengthened with metal strips, was fitted to a head which had a spike at the tip, a thickened spike at the back, and a four-pointed hammer-head. Below the head was a rondel which gave some protection to the hand. Later varieties of war hammers were fitted with longer, slightly curved spikes and remained in use in eastern Europe after they had been abandoned in the West.

Maces had similar shafts with rondels to protect the hand. Heads were still composed of flanges, often somewhat triangular in shape, again with the purpose of bringing maximum impact to a minimum area. The grips of hammers and maces were often leather covered; when not in use these weapons were hung from the saddle-bow. War hammers could also be used in foot combat, but the mace was only wielded on horseback.

(*This page*) horsemen favored the war hammer, with its stout pick-point for piercing armor. (*Opposite*) flanged maces (*top*), an early halberd (*bottom left*), and a glaive (*bottom right*).

81

SIXTEENTH CENTURY

Close helmets

Old-fashioned helmets continued to be worn long after new styles appeared, and during the sixteenth century many helmets popular in the preceding century were still in use. Kettle hats remained popular and, for the wealthier soldiers, armets were still normal wear. In the case of helmets with moveable visors or cheek-pieces, some form of holding device —spring catch, hooks, or screws—was normal from the beginning of the century. Nearly all helmets had larger combs. German armets were often made with a special rim that fitted over a raised ridge on the collar of the armor, so that they were free to rotate but were otherwise firmly in position.

However, the armet was displaced in the sixteenth century by various forms of an outwardly similar helmet, the close helmet. In the armet the face was primarily protected by the hinged side plates, and the visor guarded the slot left for

Close helmets replaced the armet during the sixteenth century. Some were especially made for the tilt and some for war; some were extremely grotesque. (*Opposite*) 1. Italian (*c.* 1510). 2. German (*c.* 1530). 3. German (*c.* 1560). 4. German (*c.* 1515). (*This page*) German helmets: 1. 1511–14; 2. *c.* 1545; 3. *c.* 1530

vision, but in the close helmet the face was covered by a bevor attached to the helmet in such a way that it could be swung upward, clear of the face. Pivoted at the same point was a visor which could be moved independent of the bevor; on some helmets the visor was made in two pieces.

To put on the close helmet, both visor and bevor were pushed up over the brow, the head was positioned inside the skull, and the bevor then lowered and locked into place, often with a spring catch. When danger became acute, the visor could be lowered to cover the face. On some close helmets a fork-like bar was attached to the bevor, so that the visor could be held safely in the open position. The visor was produced in a variety of shapes, including some versions of human or grotesque faces. About 1540 the visor was separated into two parts, and this style became general. Most early close-helmet visors projected forward to a marked degree, but later in the century this feature was greatly reduced.

During the second quarter of the sixteenth century gorget

plates were often fitted to the necks of close helmets. Many of these helmets were decorated with engraved patterns, and on a few expensive examples there might be some gold inlay work. As with other styles of helmet the inside was lined and padded to reduce the shock from any blows. Similar helmets were produced in Italy, Germany, and England.

Maximilian armor
Germany and Italy were the two main armor-producing countries of Europe, with their main centers at Innsbruck, Augsburg, Nuremberg, and Milan. Each country tended to develop individual styles, but each, in turn, was influenced by the other. Early Italian armor tended to be rounded and plain,

Both armors exhibit the common features of the Maximilian style, with the lines of fluting covering the greater part of the surface. They date from about 1540 and were made in Nuremberg.

while German armor had the slender, spiky, Gothic style.

During the first 30 years of the sixteenth century German armorers produced another style, usually known as Maximilian, after the emperor who encouraged their manufacture. Its characteristic feature was a series of ridges over the entire surface, except for the greaves, which were always left plain. On early examples the fluting was comparatively wide apart, but later on the ribs were closely spaced. Edges of individual items of armor were turned and decorated with a spiral pattern called roping. Many of the Maximilian armors were fitted with mitten gauntlets, which had no individual fingers but a series of plates to guard the back of the hand. Helmets on these armors were often of the bellows-type, with a visor which had a series of curved 'steps'.

Maximilian armors were not identical; as with these three (c. 1520), the detail varies.

Greenwich armor

Armor was made in England, but little is known about it before Henry VIII's reign. Many European sovereigns had established centers of production, and perhaps Henry felt England should have one too. Production of armor in England had previously been both inferior and insufficient for normal demands. When English nobles required good armor, they sent abroad for it. Henry had a small group of armorers from Italy and Flanders working for him at Greenwich, a small village just outside London, and in 1515 he arranged for German armorers to join them. By this time armor was in decline since the weapons of bowman, halberdier, and gunner could pierce even the best armor.

Greenwich armors were for war and the tilt. Two of Henry VIII's suits, dated 1527 (*right*) and 1540 (*left*)

Mongols and Turks against European knights

The thirteenth and fourteenth centuries were marked by the repeated defeats of European knights by the horse archers of Asia. These were victories won by superior discipline and tactics rather than superior weapons. In 1238 the Mongols burned Kiev and Moscow; in 1241 King Bela and the Hungarian knights went down near Mohacs; the Poles and the German knights fell at Liegnitz; Vienna saw the Mongol standards, and Budapest was stormed by Asian hordes. In 1291 Acre, the last stronghold of the Crusaders, fell to al-Kamil, the Mameluke leader. The Turks entered Europe in 1320, destroyed the Serbian feudal array in 1389 at Kossovo, smashed the last attempt at a European crusade at Nicopolos in 1396, took Constantinople in 1453 and advanced as far as Vienna by 1529.

To win these victories, the main weapon used was the Asiatic compound bow, backed up by a light lance and the curved scimitar. Mongol armor was made of boiled and lacquered leather while Tartars and Turks wore chain armor.

This warfare left permanent traces in European armament. The curved cavalry saber, kettle drums, the uniforms, and the light lances of 'Uhlan' and 'Hussar' regiments all show the influence of these wars against Asian light horsemen.

A Turkish spahi of the 14th century

Hunting

Egyptian wall paintings show many hunting scenes in which the longbow plays a prominent part. Assyrian kings delighted to hunt the lion and chased it in their great war chariots, dispatching it with arrows. Alexander the Great was a keen hunter and on his campaigns found time to spear wild boar, which were regarded, like lions, as the king's special prey. Spartans also hunted the wild boar.

In Britain, the Romans and Saxons do not appear to have been keen hunters, although records indicate that some sport was undertaken. The Normans brought with them a much keener interest in blood sports, and forest laws controlling great areas of country ensured that the king enjoyed good hunting. Under medieval protocol animals known as 'beasts of the forests' could only be hunted by the king or people with royal permission. These creatures were certain kinds of deer and the wild boar, of whom it was rightly said 'he could slit a man from knee to breast with one sweep of his tusks'.

To take a charging boar with a spear required nerve and a stout staff, and boar spears had thick staves with strong heads. Some hunted the boar with swords, and these too had thick, strengthened blades. Both spears and swords often had the blade pierced by a cross-bar intended to prevent too deep a penetration by the point. For safer hunting a missile weapon was used, and although the longbow was employed it was not an amateur's weapon and the crossbow was more commonly used. It could be prepared and then discharged at will, whereas the longbow had to be drawn and shot as the quarry appeared. Many of the crossbows were beautifully decorated with inlay of horn and ivory, but they were, nevertheless, immensely powerful weapons. The bow was so strong that it could not be bent by hand, and various mechanical devices such as the goat's-foot lever, the windlass, and the cranequin had to be used to span it. The short arrows, known as bolts, had tremendous penetration. Crossbows continued to be used as a hunting weapon until well into the nineteenth century, although later ones shot stones or clay balls rather than bolts.

(*Opposite top*) sixteenth-century crossbow and cranequin.
(*Bottom*) boar swords and spears had stop bars to prevent deep penetration.

Swords and daggers

It was during the sixteenth century, with the evolution of distinct civilian and military styles, that specialization began. Although firearms were the important innovation, the newest weapons did not oust established ones such as the halberd and the partizan. The head of the halberd was, however, slightly different from that of earlier models.

Military swords were not dissimilar to the earlier styles, with a double-edged, slightly tapered blade and a simple cross-guard, usually slightly down-drooping toward the blade. A number of extra guards in the form of rings and loops were often added to the cross-guard. For civilian wear the rapier became very popular, as did an Italian weapon known as the *cinquedea*. Many civilian swords had extremely elaborate hilts, featuring every type of decoration.

Daggers were worn by most gentlemen, and one elaborate style was named 'Holbein' after this artist's designs for daggers and sheaths. The elaborate sheath was often made to hold two small knives as well as the dagger. Other daggers were simpler and in general shape resembled miniature war swords, with slightly down-curving quillons, often with the hilts bound in wire. Another simple dagger, which had been popular since the fourteenth century, was the ballock dagger.

(*Opposite*) during the sixteenth century hilts became more complex, with an increasing number of rings and loops to protect the hand. Blades were larger, and the use of the point was emphasized more.

(*Above*) dagger and companion knives (1585). (*Below*) a *cinquedea* (c. 1490), popular in Italy

91

Landsknechts

Swiss mercenaries with their long pikes enjoyed a period of unbroken success, and military leaders in many countries sought means to overcome their method of fighting. Emperor Maximilian I of Austria (1493–1519) recruited a body of German pikemen and halberdiers known as *Landsknechts,* and these mercenaries proved themselves ferocious and stubborn fighters. They delighted in elaborate and extravagant dress with slashing, bunches of ribbons, wide-brimmed hats, plumes, and every form of foppery, but these tastes in no way prevented them from fighting bravely.

One of their weapons was the two-handed sword standing more than five-and-a-half feet high. Blades were of two forms —either straight-sided or flamboyant, with a wavy edge. Although the grip was big enough to be held in two hands, there was also a long, leather-covered ricasso, so that the blade itself could be grasped and the effective length of the weapon reduced for close-in work. Just below this ricasso there were often two lugs designed to protect the hand from an enemy blade slipping along the edge.

Members of these troops of *Landsknechts* fought with firearms, spears, two-handed swords, and halberds, but almost every one carried a short fighting sword in addition to the main weapon. Blades were wide and double-edged, and the swords were primarily intended for slashing rather than stabbing. Grips were simple, leather-covered, and widened gradually from the cross-guard to the pommel, which was usually dome-shaped. Guards had a characteristic shape, with the two bars folded back into an S, often terminating with a simple knob. Many of the blades had various marks inlaid in copper, and similar marks also decorated the S-shaped guards. The scabbards were usually extremely plain and often had a pocket at the top to hold a small knife.

Landsknecht armor was very simple, with a rounded breastplate, and leg defenses reached only to the knee. The shoulders were protected by curved lames, although many of the troops wore wide mail capes which covered the neck, shoulders, and tops of the arms. Light, open-faced helmets were worn by some, while others favored a close-fitting skull-cap with a peak.

92

(*Above*) much favored by the *Landsknecht* were the great two-handed swords of the sixteenth century.

(*Left*) as well as a large sword or musket the *Landsknechts* carried a sword with characteristic S-shaped quillons (*right*). They wore corselets which were usually fairly simple.

93

Gunpowder and guns

A weak form of gunpowder was known in China as far back as the eleventh century, but knowledge of this mixture spread only slowly. It is not known for certain when gunpowder first reached Europe, but its existence was recorded by Roger Bacon in the thirteenth century, for he gives what is usually accepted as a formula for its manufacture—a mixture of saltpeter, charcoal, and sulphur in varying proportions. This black powder burned rapidly, produced a cloud of smoke, a loud explosion and, if used in a gun, could propel a projectile some distance.

Gunpowder in firearms seems to have occurred early in the fourteenth century, for there are references to cannon in Italy in 1326. At first its use was restricted to siege work, and it was unreliable and highly dangerous to user as well as target. Once the idea of sending a missile some distance had been established, however, it was not long before the principle was being applied to hand-guns. These new weapons were miniature cannons fastened onto the end of a stick. Both cannons and hand-guns were fired by igniting the powder by way of a small hole drilled in the barrel.

Early hand-guns were hooked over the edge of a wall and fired by means of a hot coal, wire, or ember of wood. However, this method seriously restricted the free movement of the gunner, and the introduction of the slow-burning match was a welcome improvement. The saltpeter-impregnated cord burned slowly with a glowing end and, barring accidents, would continue to burn for some time, giving the gunner freedom to move some distance away from the fire.

Early firearms were crude but marked a new era in warfare: (*top*) bronze hand-gun; (*bottom*) large siege cannon.

Fourteenth-century hand-gun

Fifteenth-century matchlock

Sixteenth-century hackbut

Sixteenth-century hackbut

Sixteenth-century matchlock

German matchlock (1537)

NOT TO SCALE   Italian matchlock (c. 1530)

In the early fifteenth century a simple, mechanical ignition system was introduced, and an S-shaped lever, the serpentine, was fixed to the side of the stock, the wooden body-frame. Pressure on the lower section swung the top section down to press the glowing end into the powder around the touch hole, thereby igniting the main charge to fire the gun. The shape of the wooden stock was altered to make a shoulder rest, the butt, and by the sixteenth century the musket, a hand-gun with these features, was being used by most European armies.

Gunpowder changed the whole balance of power on the battlefield. The armored knight was no longer secure, for with little or no practice and a degree of luck the rawest recruit could kill the greatest in the land.

Armor

During the sixteenth century armors became at the same time technically outstanding and defensively inefficient. Many were decorated with superb skill, but toward the end of the century surfaces were often no longer smooth or shaped to deflect the blow quite so easily. Heavy cavalry still wore full armor with close helmets or armets. Shoulder defenses were strengthened by the addition of haute pieces, plates that stood vertically from the shoulders to give extra protection to the throat. Breast-plates had a central ridge, and two fairly large tassets hung over the thighs. Foot defenses no longer had pointed toes but followed the civilian style, with very broad toes. Light cavalry wore no leg armor at all and,

(*Left*) armor from Nuremberg, the burgonet being fitted with a barred visor (1540). (*Right*) Milanese armor (1510–15), still with a mail skirt

Sixteenth-century boot stirrups

unlike the heavy cavalry, their horses were completely unarmored. Many foot soldiers wore only a light helmet and a jacket reinforced with metal plates, a brigandine or jack.

Armor was being rendered obsolete by the development of firearms. Although it was quite possible to make armor strong enough to resist a bullet, the weight became excessive, and during the second half of the sixteenth century there was a growing tendency for it to be discarded. At first only the leg defenses went, but by the end of the century the only armor worn by many troops was a helmet and a breast-plate.

In the sixteenth century highly decorative armor was fashionable: (*left*) Augsburg parade armor (*c.* 1510); (*right*) Emperor Charles V's armor.

97

Half armor

During the sixteenth and seventeenth centuries there was an increasing emphasis on quick movement. In place of the heavy, slow-moving cavalry of an earlier period there were quick-moving cavalry. Many wore only a corselet comprising a light helmet and a breast- and back-plate, as well as, perhaps, arm defenses. Many infantry were similarly equipped. Records of the period often speak of armor known as Almain rivet, which was apparently a mass-produced half armor. Most corselets and Almain rivets comprised a collar, breast- and back-plates, tassets, and open helmet, arm defenses, and gauntlets. Some lacked gauntlets but had an extension of plate over the back of the hand. To accommodate different sizes there was a sliding pin in the arm defenses.

A half armor usually described as Pisan was produced in Italy, mostly in Milan. It comprised an open-faced helmet (a burgonet), a breast- and back-plate, and hung from the waist two tassets which looked like a series of lames but were

Half armors: 1. mid-sixteenth century, German black-and-white; 2. Innsbruck (1555)

1

2

98

made in fact from single pieces. Full arm defenses were fitted, complete with elbow couters which extended around the arm. The gauntlets had wide, sweeping cuffs. This armor was frequently etched with bands of decoration. Although it looked impressive, the quality was poor, and the helmets were often not very sturdy. Some German armors comprising breast- and backplates, helmet, and tassets were painted with black, rust-resisting paint and known as black-and-white armors.

Later examples: 1. Italian (1580–90); 2. black-and-white (c. 1590); 3. Pisan or N. Italian (1560–70)

Parade armor

As the demand for war armor began to diminish the master armorers, no doubt, sought other outlets for their products. One profitable line was that of parade armors. Naturally, only the wealthy could afford these luxuries, for such armors were elaborate and made with little or no restriction on cost. The first manifestation of this trend can be seen in the grotesque visors which appeared about 1510. These visors— molded into human faces, bird and animal heads—are superb examples of the armorer's skill, but their very shape defeats their prime purpose, for the projections would have held the edge of the blade rather than deflected it.

Superb technique is also illustrated in the armor made to look like civilian dress, with its metal puffing and slashing. Embossing (the hammering out of decoration into relief) was practiced by Italian and German armorers, and some of the most outstanding examples of such work were the helmets produced by Filippo Negroli of Milan.

Other styles of decoration were also used to embellish the armors of the mighty. Such armors were attractive and, no doubt, created quite an impression, but rough usage must have spoiled much of the decoration. Painting was used on helmets from the thirteenth to the sixteenth century and there are references to painted body armor in the fourteenth century, but this fashion fell out of favor early in the 1500's.

Etching was used until the seventeenth century; this was done by covering the surface of the metal with paint or wax and scratching the desired picture or pattern through the wax. The plate was then covered with acid and all surfaces not protected by the paint or wax were attacked. In Germany, a process which was just the reverse was adopted during the sixteenth century; here the required design was painted onto the metal so that it was left untouched by the acid and stood away from the etched surface. On some armors the etched areas were covered with a thin layer of colored enamel, but this seems to have been a rarely used technique.

Engraving was occasionally used, the metal being cut with a sharp, pointed tool. Gilding was done by covering the surface with a thin layer of gold, and silvering by pressing thin layers of silver foil onto roughened surfaces.

Superbly embossed helmets by
Negroli of Milan (1530–40)

Finely embossed armors: made
(*above*) at Innsbruck (*c.* 1555)
in the style of civilian dress,
and (*right*), at Augsburg (*c.* 1530)

101

To resist bullets, armor was made thicker and heavier. During the seventeenth century a type of armor composed of a fairly substantial breast-plate, long, laminated tassets reaching to the knees, and a burgonet (usually fitted with a barred visor) was worn by the heavy cavalry. It was usually described as cuirassier's armor and was largely abandoned by the middle of the century.

SEVENTEENTH CENTURY

Cuirassiers

Although the custom of wearing armor was diminishing during the sixteenth century, it was not completely discarded until World War I. Some heavily armored troops were used during the English Civil War (1642–48) and the Thirty Years War in Europe (1618–48). One type of soldier was known as a cuirassier, and he wore comparatively heavy armor. On his head he wore a close helmet, fitted with a peak and a barred visor in place of the more usual plate type; however, a number of troops still wore the conventional close helmet with full visor.

An additional form of close helmet, which appeared at the turn of the century in Italy, was the type referred to as a Savoyard. It had a visor with holes pierced for eyes, nose and mouth, and its skull-like appearance also earned it the name *Totenkopf* (death's head). Cuirassiers had mostly abandoned the use of the lance and now relied upon a good sword and a brace of pistols fitted with a new device for firing the powder, the wheel-lock. The pistols were carried in a pair of holsters at the saddle-bow.

As well as the close helmet, the cuirassier wore a three-quarter armor reaching to the knees. Greaves and shoes were discarded in favor of high, leather boots. From the waist to the knees long tassets composed of many lames were worn, terminating in a poleyn and secured at the top to the lower edge of the breast-plate by straps or by turning pins which engaged with slots on the tassets. Pauldrons and vambraces (armor for the arm) were usually united into one flexible piece, with the inside of the elbow protected by small, overlapping plates; gauntlets completed the arm defenses.

Breast-plates were flat, although many men still wore the older style, the peascod, with a central ridge terminating in a small, down-drawn point at the center of the waist. The armor of many cuirassiers was dark, and the rivets securing the numerous lames were brass headed, lending an attractive feature to what was otherwise quite a heavy, clumsy-looking armor. Their helmets usually had large gorget plates which extended down well over the chest.

English Civil War armor and weapons

The seventeenth century saw the general abandonment of armor by the foot soldier; it lingered on for a while in the cavalry, where the soldiers retained their breast- and backplates until the eighteenth century. One result of the English Civil War was the better orgainzation of the arms trade in Britain: pressure of war revealed that the old system could not meet demand. Gunpowder made a nearly complete sweep of battlefield weapons; the matchlock musket and bayonet held sway, although the sword and, for a while, the pike were retained—only survivors of the armory of staff and edged weapons. Cavalry relied on their swords and pistols, whereas the foot soldier had his musket and sword. For most of the Civil War the pike was given a new role in the hands of the pikeman, whose job it was to protect the musketeers at their

2

4

most vulnerable moment—when they were reloading.

Pikemen wore breast- and back-plates with wide, skirt-like tassets which looked as if they were fashioned from several lames but were, in fact, single plates made to resemble the older style. Breast- and back-plates were held in place by belts and straps which were often covered with small, overlapping, metal plates to reduce the risk of their being cut. Gloves were normally worn to protect the hands from being rubbed by the long, ash shafts of the pike. Cavalry wore somewhat similar breast- and back-plates over a thick, buff leather coat strong enough to turn aside a sword cut. To guard the vulnerable left hand, which held the bridle, a gauntlet with a cuff to the elbow was worn. A few cuirassiers served in full armor, but they were not a great success: one group of Parliamentarians was called 'a regiment of lobsters'.

Unlike musketeers (1), pikemen wore substantial armor (2), while cavalrymen wore a heavy cuirassier's armor (3) or a buff coat, breast- and back-plates, and bridle gauntlet (4), that shown belonged to James II.

1

3

(*Left*) a typical, three-barred 'pot' worn by cavalry on both sides in the Civil War. The peak was pivoted. (*Below*) a morion of Philip IV of Spain (*c.* 1626): note the plume-holder

(*Left*) a helmet of German origin with a single-bar nasal

English Civil War helmets

Possibly the most characteristic helmet of the English Civil War was the 'lobster-tail pot', worn by the cavalry of both sides. There were two varieties, which differed largely in the provisions made for face protection; those made on the continent, usually in the Low Countries, had a single-bar nasal which could be raised or lowered, whereas the English variety had a three-bar arrangement attached to the pivoted peak, and this entire section could be raised or lowered. Pikemen wore either a wide-brimmed pot or a Spanish morion, also called a cabasset. All these helmets usually had earflaps which tied beneath the chin. Many had a small metal tube riveted onto the back just above the brim; this served as a plume-holder, colored plumes being used for identification. After the middle of the sixteenth century many helmets were constructed from two pieces of metal joined together: a far easier method than fashioning them from a single piece.

Cavalrymen, especially Royalist soldiers, sometimes scorned a helmet and compromised by wearing a steel skull-cap beneath their usual wide-brimmed hats. The caps, secretes, were very similar to those worn under mail many centuries earlier. A few examples of steel hats copying the civilian style are known, but these were presumably made to special order for wealthier soldiers. Some very heavy and thick-walled burgonets were made, but these were intended for siege operations and were worn only for quite limited periods.

Helmets and armor of this and earlier periods were often proved, that is tested to ensure that they could stop a bullet. Most of the 'bullet' marks seen on armor are, in fact, the result of proving and not of action. Armor was described as being musket-, caliver-, or pistol-proof, indicating that it might be expected to resist these various weapons. In earlier times the proving was done with the crossbow. It was, of course, normal for the breast-plate to be much thicker than the back-plate or other pieces, and most helmets were only pistol-proof.

(*Right*) a steel helmet shaped like a civilian hat, plus an adjustable nasal. (*Below*) a German single-bar pot. Both *c.* 1640

(*Right*) an Italian Savoyard helmet with the visor, which was fashioned like a face, held locked in place by a side hook (*c.* 1600)

Weapons

A great variety of swords was used during the seventeenth century, including several which had evolved from earlier models. The most common, certainly in Britain, was the cavalry broadsword. Fitted with blades of varying widths, sometimes two or three inches wide, it had several short fullers just below the guard. Hilts were quite elaborate, a series of bars springing from the pommel and ending below the grip to form a basket to protect the hand. Often the bars were chiseled; many had a head believed to be a death mask of Charles I cut into them which gained the swords the title of mortuary swords.

Infantry swords tended to be somewhat similar in design, with far fewer bars, but often featured a shell-guard, which was a metal plate fitting into a loop at the bottom of the grip. Many had a loop on the right side called a thumb-ring, through which the thumb was passed to ensure a good grip.

Rapiers and broadswords were the swords most generally used during the first half of the seventeenth century. Most of them had hilts which were simpler in design than previously.

As the musket and pistol developed, many older types of weapon were discarded or relegated to ceremonial duty. This is particularly true of staff weapons such as glaives, halberds, and partizans. Many were produced with highly decorative blades, often bearing the owner's coat-of-arms. Blades were also gilded and pierced, and certain features were so exaggerated that they lost any practical use. Shafts were often covered with velvet, and fringes were fitted below the heads, although some earlier, more practical, weapons were similarly treated to prevent rain or sweat making the shafts slippery.

In eastern Europe changes tended to come much later, and certain pole-arms and weapons such as the war hammer were still used after western Europe had abandoned them. The wearing of armor also lingered on in eastern Europe. The lance was abandoned after the Thirty Years War and was not revived until the eighteenth century when Napoleon incorporated some Polish lancers into his army and started a new fashion.

Cavalry picks were still used, but most pole-arms had become less practical, being mainly for ceremonial purposes and bodyguards.

Rapiers

Early sword-play was a matter of slashing, parrying, and brute strength or quick stabs with the *estoc*. War swords were often used with a two-handed grip and were known as hand-and-a-half swords. As the custom of hooking the forefinger over the crossguard became more common, there was need to protect the finger, and loops were added to the hilt. Moreover, as armor was worn much less frequently, swords became lighter, and there was a much greater emphasis on the use of the point.

All these factors combined to produce the rapier, which probably first emerged in Spain. The term is recorded as early as 1474 and derived from *espada ropera*, a dress or costume sword. About 1550 the term was applied to a light cut-and-thrust sword used mostly by civilians, with a long, two-edged blade and a guard of bars and loops.

From about 1560 a rapier meant a light, thrusting sword for fencing, a type of

As fencing increased in popularity in the late sixteenth and seventeenth centuries, rapiers became very common. Hilts vary greatly in the number and arrangement of bars and guards.

sword-play which had developed in Italy and spread into most of Europe. Blades were, at first, very long—up to five feet—and double-edged, but later they were soon shortened to more manageable proportions. Hilts became more complex, and by about 1570 they had acquired the style known as swept hilt. At the same time some of the lower rings were fitted with plates, often pierced, which were later enlarged to form two round shells. Swords with such hilts were called Pappenheimers after a commander in the Thirty Years War. In England the bottom rings were often replaced by two cup-like plates, often featuring inlaid silver decoration. All this culminated in the appearance of the cup-hilt rapier in the second quarter of the seventeenth century. It was popular in Italy and Spain, where it was used until well into the eighteenth century. However, during the seventeenth century blades were becoming shorter and hilts simpler as the small-sword evolved.

During the second quarter of the seventeenth century the bars on the hilt were often replaced by a cup with long quillons. This cup-hilted rapier was especially popular in Spain and Italy.

Daggers were common wear during the seventeenth century, and some were used in the left hand as an auxiliary weapon in fencing.

Left-hand daggers

Daggers were never a prime military weapon but were carried by most soldiers and civilians for self-protection against assassins. During the sixteenth century the quillon dagger, which was more or less a miniature version of the full-sized sword, came into general use in a variety of forms, some extremely decorative, with chiseled pommels and quillons. The type first appeared in the thirteenth century and has been in use ever since.

As fencing developed, the increasing emphasis on the use of the point stimulated the Masters of Fence to devise means whereby the fencer might guard himself against the point of his opponent's sword. The general aim was to parry, or knock aside, an opponent's blade. It was done with the sword blade or by an auxiliary device. Some teachers advocated the use of a mailed gauntlet to grasp the blade; others, a cloak around the arm as a simple shield. However, one of the most popular aids was a dagger used, point upward, in the left hand.

Quillon daggers were used in this way to catch and divert

the point of the rapier; to give extra protection, a ring was mounted on the quillon block. Most of these daggers have a substantial ricasso, so that the ball of the thumb could be pressed down on the blade to ensure a firm grip. The quillons were often curved slightly downward and forward to offer a little extra protection to the hand. Many such daggers were made *en suite,* in the same style as the companion rapier and decorated in the same fashion. Blades were usually stiff, and some earlier versions are ribbed and pierced.

Fencing with left-hand daggers enjoyed a vogue until about 1630. After that, left-hand daggers were gradually discarded, except in Spain and Italy where they were popular until well into the eighteenth century. Spain developed a type with long, thin quillons and a shell-guard springing from the quillon and tapering up to the pommel. A slight depression on the broad ricasso took the ball of the thumb. The blade often had a series of notches designed to catch the opponent's blade, and a few had teeth to catch, hold, or break a blade.

Spanish left-hand daggers were distinguished by large hand-guards. Notched edges were sometimes fitted to catch or break a blade.

Hunting swords and hangers

Hunting retained its popularity throughout the Middle Ages and continued to be enjoyed by many of the leisured classes during the seventeenth and eighteenth centuries. All the traditional weapons, including the crossbow, were still used, but during the seventeenth century a short sword was usually carried by the hunter. Such a weapon might be referred to as a hunting sword, a hanger, or a riding sword, but the distinctions, if any, are very small. Just as travel was hazardous and some convenient sword was needed for self-defense, so in hunting a short sword was handy for dispatching wounded game; on both occasions the weapon used could be called a

These general-purpose swords were known as riding swords, hangers, or hunting swords. Many have hilts of staghorn with a side shell.

hanger. The distinguishing characteristic of this group of swords is that their blades are curved, an unusual feature as most European swords—apart from the falchion, in use from the early thirteenth century—were straight-bladed.

Hangers were almost invariably simple in design and construction. In general they were short, with a blade that seldom exceeded two feet or so in length. Blades of the seventeenth century were slightly curved, single-edged, and of sturdy construction. It was not uncommon for them to have some mark stamped on them; this was the trademark of the cutler, each of whom had his own device, initials, or emblem with which all his goods were marked.

Hilts varied in detail, but basically they consisted of a grip, usually of stag's horn, a simple knuckle-bow, and a short, down-curved back quillon. Many had a side shell which often carried a scene of hunting or mythology. There was no pommel, but simply a cap to top the horn grip and hold the end of the knuckle-bow. Guards were usually of brass, sometimes of steel; the few intricate ones were obvious exceptions. Scabbards were generally of leather, often plain but occasionally with a simple decoration of incised lines. Fittings were of brass or steel, frequently to match the knuckle-bow, and a long prong attached the weapon to the belt or sling.

Italian falchion, dated 1618

Sixteenth-century falchion

German hanger (c. 1640)

English hanger (1750–51)

English, saw-backed hanger

115

Bayonets and stilettos

Gunpowder certainly altered the emphasis and balance of warfare and may, with justification, be described as the initiator of technological warfare. However, there were drawbacks and problems for the gunners and musketeers. Not least among these was the powder itself, which tended to be variable in quality and uncertain in performance. Gunners had to be able to calculate the amount of powder required to throw a certain size of shot a certain distance, and it was appreciated that it was not always convenient for a soldier to carry a book of tables. One solution was to use the gunner's stiletto, which served the double purpose of dagger and calculator; the sides of the triangular blade were marked off with sundry tables to assist the master gunner in his calculations. Most gunners' stillettos had a simple cross-hilt and were fashioned completely of metal; many were of Italian origin.

For the musketeer the problems were less academic and far more serious: having fired his musket he was then defenseless, with a heavy and cumbersome weapon in his hands, until he had reloaded. One solution was to guard him with groups of pikemen, but this wasted man-power, and around the middle of the seventeenth century another method was evolved whereby the useless musket could be converted into a short pike to hold off the cavalry. This conversion was simple and was achieved by pushing a knife, hilt first, into the barrel. Thus the bayonet was created, although the same name had earlier been applied to a knife made at Bayonne in France.

Obviously the bayonet imposed limitations, for with it in position it was impossible to load or fire the musket. Attempts to overcome this were soon in hand, and a fitting using lugs enabled the bayonet to be fastened onto the outside of the barrel. The most successful system, however, was that using a tubular socket which dropped over the barrel and was then held in position by a stud or, later, a spring clip. This system evolved late in the seventeenth century and was in general use by the mid-eighteenth. Late in the nineteenth century another system, using a stud on the side of the barrel and a groove on the hilt of the bayonet, became more common, and with minor modification this system has remained in use up to the present.

(*Below*) a seventeenth-century, English plug bayonet. (*Center*) a late seventeenth-century, all-steel gunner's stiletto, its blade marked with tables used in calculating charges of powder. (*Right*) a highly decorated, Spanish plug bayonet, probably a hunting weapon (*c.* 1770)

Small-swords

Rapiers were popular during the first half of the seventeenth century, but as towns became more crowded there was less room for extravagant fashions and this long-bladed weapon was gradually abandoned. New types of sword, shorter, lighter, and more convenient for town wear, were evolved. From about 1630 the length of the blade was gradually reduced, and the complex system of bars and loops in earlier hand-guards was modified. About the same time there appeared a type of rapier with two fairly large, saucer-like shells and two long quillons which curved down toward the point. Two arms sprang from the quillons and curved to meet the inside base of the shells; there was often no knuckle-bow.

By the middle of the century most blades were about 30 inches long. Quillons and the arms of the hilt were shortened, and many swords were fitted with smaller shells. Not only were the shells made smaller but they were also flattened and, at a later date, lost their raised borders. This was the basic form of the small-sword, and much decorative skill was lavished on it, with chiseling of the hilt, silver inlay, and later hilts sometimes fashioned completely of silver.

Another type of sword popular toward the end of the seventeenth century was the pillow-sword with its simple hilt of two quillons and perhaps a side ring. Dish-hilt rapiers were primarily dueling weapons with large, flat dish-guards.

Small-swords became part of gentlemen's everyday costume and were to remain so for a century, with the style basically unchanged. In the last quarter of the seventeenth century the knuckle-bow was once again common on these swords, and the quillons were reduced still further in size. By the turn of the century the forward quillon below the knuckle-bow had largely been abandoned, while the rear one was reduced to a short, bulbous termination extending only a little beyond the shells. Pommels became more egg-shaped, and the grips were generally square or oval in section, thick at the center and tapering toward both ends. Many grips were bound with wire, which not only looked attractive but ensured a firm hold. Blades were generally double-edged and tapered to a sharp point.

In general, seventeenth-century swords had simple hilts with wire-bound grips, and many had some high-relief decoration.

EIGHTEENTH CENTURY

Hangers

Hangers continued in fashion throughout the eighteenth century and, as a broad generalization, it may be said that they tended to become more elaborate. Some retained the curved blade, but straight blades were far more common and these were often etched. Hilts varied greatly in design, and many dating from the early part of the century have shells projecting sideways or downward, parallel with the blade.

Knuckle-bows were retained on some swords, but others had only short quillons, sometimes with a decorative chain linking the front quillon with the cap. Grips were of wood, horn, stained ivory, or wood covered with a thin layer of tortoise-shell. A few hangers were made with a flintlock pistol fitted to the hilt and partially covered by the side shell. Sheaths were still made of leather, although the mounts were a

The majority of eighteenth-century hunting swords were fitted with straight blades and hilts of brass. Some grips were made of stag's horn, see the detail (*left*), but others had a covering of tortoise-shell.

little more elaborate, many European examples being fitted with a pocket which held a knife and fork. In Germany hunters carried hangers until the twentieth century.

Hunting during the seventeenth and eighteenth centuries retained its popularity, and most of those taking part carried one form or other of the typical hunting swords. However, among the servants of the hunt one, at least, would have carried the elaborate wood-knife, which is also known as the *trousse de chasse*. This complete kit was housed in an elaborate metal-and-leather sheath and comprised the equipment required to dispatch and dismember the kill—usually a stag or boar. The largest of the items was a broad-bladed, heavy, cleaver-like knife. Most *trousses* had a variety of more usual knives, forks, and bodkins, and these were used in cutting up the carcass. Many of the wood-knives that have survived belonged to monarchs and princes and, as befits such princely possessions, they bear the arms of the owner and are decorated with ivory, and with gilt and silver.

Somewhat similar to the large cleaver were the elaborate knives called *présentoir*, used as their French name implies in the serving of food at table. They had a wide, flat blade with a handle often set in the center of the blade.

A German wood-knife (*c.* 1770), a complete set of implements in a single sheath for dispatching and dismembering the quarry

Small-swords

Every man with any pretensions to quality wore a sword in town; this practice continued until about 1780 when the sword, as an article of everyday wear, was generally abandoned. Considerable sums of money were expended on these delicate but deadly weapons and, although there are numerous variations in detail, the basic style remained unaltered.

Knuckle-bows were common until the end of the period, when some of the dress swords had only a chain-guard like that on some hangers. Apart from this feature it is possible to date many examples by comparing certain features like shells, blades, and the arms of the hilt. Early seventeenth-century examples of the small-sword have two distinct shells, often with one larger than the other. However, as the century progressed, the two shells were more often made the same size and then combined to form a flattened figure of eight which, by the 1760's, had become an oval. It is this shape that is found on the late eighteenth- and early nineteenth-century dress swords.

Another useful feature for dating the sword is the size of the loops formed by the arms of the hilt as they curve back to meet the shells. In certain styles of fencing the fingers could be hooked over the quillon and slipped into these rings. As most wearers were primarily concerned with the appearance rather than the use of the weapon, these rings became less important and were gradually reduced in size. By the 1750's they were usually too small to accommodate the fingers; by 1780 they were little more than almost flattened bars.

One variation was the boat-shell hilt; here the two shells were united into a single heart-shape with the point curving up and splitting to accommodate the forward quillon. The Heavy Cavalry dress sword for officers, worn from 1796 to 1834, was of this style. Small-sword blades were often ground hollow and in section resembled a thin triangle with concave sides. A similar type, the *colichemarde*, had a wide top section but narrowed sharply about one-third of the way down to a very narrow, thrusting point. Every form of decoration was used to embellish small-swords, and they were carried in thin sheaths of parchment or leather-covered wood, suspended from the waistband or belt by a hanger of small chains.

(*Above*) English, silver-hilted small-sword, hallmarked 1724

(*Above*) English, all-steel small-sword (*c.* 1790), blued. (*Below*) English mourning sword with black-bound grip (*c.* 1750)

(*Left*) French small-sword with a silver hilt (*c.* 1760). (*Below*) late small-sword, with a chain replacing the solid knuckle-bow

123

NINETEENTH CENTURY

Armor

By the nineteenth century, armor had been abandoned in Britain for many years, but many European countries had retained it for their cavalry. Spain, France, and Prussia continued to equip some of their cavalry units with breast- and back-plates as a means of protection, although the practice was lessening and wars, such as the Crimean and the American Civil War, were demonstrating that armor was no longer worthwhile. It is interesting to note that the French heavy cavalry who went into battle in World War I were wearing armor and helmets that differed very little from those worn by the charging cavalry at Waterloo.

George IV, whose military interest was largely limited to uniforms, brought armor back into the British Army; he had the Household Cavalry don breast- and back-plates and, a little later, metal helmets were also adopted. Some of the helmets worn by British and foreign cavalry were highly

Some nineteenth-century armor: Danish general's helmet (*below*); British Household Cavalryman's cuirass (*right*)

decorative but totally impractical, with huge, top-heavy crests. They were, in fact, more decorative than protective, and the same applies to the Household Cavalry's armor.

Apart from the cuirass and metal helmets, which were generally limited to cavalry, the last bit of armor to survive in the British Army was the gorget. It will be remembered that originally this was worn to protect the neck, but when the main body armor was discarded during the seventeeth century some gorgets were retained and became formalized into large, decorative, crescent-shaped pieces of metal hung around the neck. During the eighteenth century they became smaller and far less decorative. Most were of gilt brass, but some were of silver; all bore some engraving. Most bore the royal cypher, and some the regimental number.

In 1796 it was ordered that all gorgets should bear the royal cypher and a wreath, and this remained the basic style until they were finally abolished in 1830. Gorgets were suspended around the neck by a length of ribbon and were worn only by officers, as a badge of rank. Elsewhere in Europe the practice of wearing gorgets continued to a much later date, and during the Third Reich the Germans revived the practice.

References in eighteenth-century military books to breastplates do not, as a rule, mean a cuirass but the small, decorative plate worn on the cross-straps at the chest and now called a shoulder-belt plate. It was abandoned in 1855.

British officer's gorget

Bayonets

During the nineteenth century the bayonet was still regarded as a useful device, and many versions were produced. If there was any general trend, it was toward an increase in the length. Many had blades up to three feet long, although this type was really an attempt to produce a sword-bayonet—a weapon which could be fitted onto the end of a barrel or used as a separate sword.

Early in the nineteenth century a rifle designed by a London gunsmith, Ezekiel Baker, was adopted by the British Army. It had a brass-hilted bayonet which engaged with a bar on the side of the barrel. This was an uncommon method of attachment; most long-arms still used a socket fitting. About the middle of the nineteenth century a stud, on the side of the barrel, which engaged with a slot in the bayonet grip became the usual method of attachment. There was a fashion for *yataghan* bayonets, with curved blades, about the same time.

As firearms became more

Bayonets: 1 & 2. German Mausers, patterns 1871 and 1898; 3. British Lee Metford (*c.* 1890)

sophisticated, with magazines holding several cartridges, the bayonet, never a convenient weapon, became far less important. It was shorter, and the stud-and-socket fitting became more or less universal. Blades were straight, although their section was not always conventional. The Lebel had a blade with a cruciform section, and some later Enfield bayonets were like long bodkins.

In addition to bayonets some troops carried a short side-arm which, in the case of engineers and associated troops, often had a saw-edged back to the blade. With this the side-arm became a tool as well as a weapon. A number of special weapons were produced, such as the Elcho bayonet, used during the Ashanti War in 1873 to fit on the Snider rifle. It had a straight, saw-backed blade which widened about half-way along into a spear-head shape and was intended as a useful aid in clearing brush and wood. It must, however, have been point-heavy; in any case it was soon withdrawn from service.

Bayonets with unusual blades: 4. French Lebel (post 1916); 5. English *yataghan* (c. 1860)

Uniforms and weapons

During the nineteenth century Europe's army uniforms were at their most splendid. They were a rainbow of colors and a profusion of gold braid, loops, spare jackets, and similar fripperies. This extravagant style had originally been set by the Imperial Army of Napoleon, and other nations followed suit by copying, improving, and embellishing its designs. There was also a tendency for countries to copy the uniforms of the victors of any war, and even in some cases those of the vanquished. However, from the middle of the century there was a gradual simplification of uniforms, and most of the extravagances were abandoned.

Helmets were worn by many units but were primarily the prerogative of the cavalry. In Britain the helmets were impressive, if impractical; the pattern of 1822 was a so-called 'Roman' style, with a skull of thin steel decorated with gilt leaves and the royal arms and surmounted by an enormous crest of bearskin. How a rider kept the helmet on and retained

Nineteenth-century uniforms, particularly cavalry ones, were a rainbow of color and decoration. (*Left*) Spanish cuirassiers (*c.* 1845). (*Right*) officer of the British 11th Hussars (*c.* 1850)

his seat is still a mystery. Russians and Prussians favored helmets of more reasonable size but then surmounted them with large gilded or silvered eagles, horsehair plumes, or bunches of feathers.

Many cavalry units wore plain breast-plates, but others had applied decorations of stars and eagles. Cavalry swords were fairly long-bladed and usually straight or, at most, slightly curved. Most hilts were basically simple, with a guard not dissimilar to the British Gothic pattern. The sword-belt was often elaborate, with stripes and decorated buckles, and hanging from the side was the sabretache, which was originally intended as a message pouch but which soon became yet another form of decoration, with embroidered and braid cyphers and regimental crests. A brace of pistols was carried by most cavalry men, in holsters slung from the saddle.

Infantry weapons were limited to musket and bayonet for the great majority of troops, although a few carried special swords or even, occasionally, pole-arms.

(*Left*) two Russian cuirassiers (*c.* 1850). (*Right*) a French lancer of the Imperial Guard

Scottish weapons

Possibly the weapon which everybody connects with Scotland is the claymore. Strictly speaking, a claymore was a large, two-handed sword used by the Scots during the sixteenth and seventeenth centuries. A long, straight blade was fitted to a straight hilt, also very long, with two shortish, down-sloping quillons terminating in a pierced shamrock pattern. In the seventeenth century the quillons were more curved, and a large shell-plate was fitted at the side to protect the hands.

This, then, was the true 'great sword', the claymore or, in Gaelic, *claidheamh mòr*, but for the last 200 years the term has been applied to the basket-hilted broadsword. The basket-hilt probably had its beginnings in Germany and, apart from bars, often incorporated solid plates. By the seventeenth century, this full basket-hilt was in use in Scotland and has continued to be favored there until the present. The inside of the basket is fitted with a layer of leather.

Basket-hilts: 1. late seventeenth-century; 2. eighteenth-century; 3. *c.* 1800; 4. *c.* 1740

Blades are straight and double-edged and, in the past, often bore the name of Andrea Farrara, blade-maker, whose name was a guarantee of quality, pirated for years after his death.

The Scots were not the only troops to carry the basket-hilted broadsword, for some British dragoon regiments carried swords with a similar basket hand-guard. The Scots also carried a large dagger which became known as a dirk, although in the seventeenth century the term was used for some other weapon. The dirk probably developed from the older ballock dagger. Hilts were simple, with a flat top pommel and two lobes at the base where the blade joined the grip. The wood was often carved with typically Celtic, interwoven strap decoration. Blades were usually straight, tapering to a point; many early examples utilized cut-down sword blades.

In the mid-nineteenth century there was a romantic revival of all things Scottish, and numbers of dirks were made, usually with a large cairngorm set in the pommel and with a sheath fitted with pockets to hold cutlery. Small daggers worn in the sock and called *skean dhu* also seem to have originated with the revival although, no doubt, some earlier knives had been carried like this. Scottish shields were round and made of wood-covered leather reinforced with brass-headed nails.

Wood-and-leather, Scottish targe

Scottish dirks developed from the earlier ballock dagger.

131

TWENTIETH CENTURY

World War I

The Crimean War (1854–56) could well be described as the last of the picturesque wars in which uniforms were glamorous and impractical. The American Civil War (1861–65) and the Boer War (1899–1902) demonstrated beyond doubt that modern warfare left no room for frills. Most countries discarded these extravagances, as well as armor and helmets, and at the beginning of World War I most infantry were wearing soft caps. Many German units wore the *Pickelhaube*, but because it was made out of leather it gave little protection.

When fighting finally reached the terrible stalemate in the trenches, doctors found that there was a disproportionate number of head wounds. The Germans saw the need for head protection, and after advice and tests they introduced a helmet which was similar to the sallet. Its use dramatically reduced casualties, and naturally the other combatants followed suit; by 1916–

World War I helmets: 1. French, also World War II; 2. British; 3. German, modified in World War II; 4. German *Pickelhaube*

17 most troops were wearing steel helmets or 'tin hats'.

Other forms of armor were introduced from 1914–18, including a visor-like face-guard of mail for tank crews and an almost complete armor for snipers and exposed gunners. The latter was thick, heavy, and comprised a helmet reinforce and a breast-plate with simple tassets.

Trench warfare saw the introduction of raiding parties which crept across no man's land to obtain information or prisoners. For the silent, vicious fighting involved, a number of fighting, or trench, knives were developed. Many were no more than cut-down bayonets or blades crudely mounted in simple hilts, but a number were commercially produced, and some could be folded away.

Despite the emphasis on the bayonet's terrors preached by militarists, the weapon was used mostly for opening tins and as a cooking implement. If it had any purpose it was for holding off cavalry, and it became obsolete as cavalry disappeared.

World War I saw much hand-to-hand combat. Besides bayonets, many forms of fighting or trench knives were used.

133

Nazi daggers

Solingen was always a noted center for weapon production and had prospered as such. With Germany's defeat in World War I came financial disaster, with factories idle and craftsmen unemployed despite attempts to branch out into other fields. When the Nazis took control in 1933 some of these craftsmen and factory owners approached Adolf Hitler, the new German leader, with the suggestion that some form of dagger would complete the uniform of his many minions by adding a decorative but war-like touch. Since it would certainly do this and also ensure the industry's financial recovery, the Nazis agreed.

One of the most attractive styles selected was based on the Holbein dagger of the sixteenth century. This type was made with a bright steel blade etched or engraved with various mottoes. A hilt of wood was fitted to the blade, and its color determined by the unit to which it was issued. Storm-troopers of the Sturm-Abteilung wore an Holbein dagger which had a brown hilt and a matching scabbard, whereas members of the Transport Corps, the NSKK, had the same dagger but with a black sheath. The dreaded élite, the SS, had a black hilt and a black scabbard. All were usually suspended by a small leather strap passing through a ring on the scabbard.

The Luftwaffe, the German Air Force, had two different versions, both having a basically cruciform hilt with flared quillons and a grip which could be any one of a number of colors. Army officers carried a dagger similar to those worn by the Luftwaffe, although the pommels differed and the quillons had a different center figure. Naval daggers had the pommel in the form of an eagle.

Daggers were also issued to a wide range of officials, including those in the Fire Department, Customs, Air Raid Protection, Forestry, and even the Red Cross, although the latter carried a dagger with a saw back and a blunt point which could be used as a screwdriver. As well as the standard patterns there were more elaborate ones, which were for presentation models, with decorated blades and often more elaborate sheaths and hanging chains. The Germans also produced dress bayonets which looked like genuine bayonets but, in fact, could not be fitted to a rifle, being purely for show.

Hitler introduced the issue of dress weapons to many units. A popular style was based on the so-called Holbein dagger.

(*Above*) a Holbein dagger

(*Above*) NSKK

(*Above*) Nazi Navy
(*Below*) National Flying Corps

(*Below*) another Nazi dress weapon: a police bayonet

Differences between helmets were mostly only a matter of detail.

World War II

World War II saw an enormous increase in the use of armor in all forms, with many styles incorporating new materials. Steel helmets were still worn and were basically the same as those worn in World War I. The German helmet differed slightly in that the brim was not as deep as the 1916 pattern, but otherwise it was essentially the same. Special patterns were produced for parachute troops; these usually had no brim and were fitted with a double chinstrap.

Bayonets were still carried by most troops, although they were probably used even less than in World War I. The new British bayonets were far shorter, but naturally many older models from stock were still issued. Body armor was used, but again only on an extremely limited scale. Bullet-proof waistcoats were made using a form of scale armor, although here the metal plates dropped into the pockets of an overgarment and were fashioned of new metals. Armor plate was fitted

A British Cromwell
tank, 75 mm gun

World War II helmets:
1. American; 2. Russian; 3. Italian; 4. Japanese

to aircraft to offer aircrew some protection against fighters' bullets or splinters from anti-aircraft shells.

Caterpillar tracks were not a new idea and armor was many thousands of years old, but it was not until 1916 that the two ideas were combined to produce the tank. The new invention was never fully exploited in World War I, but between the wars theories of tank warfare were developed, as the Germans demonstrated in 1940, when their Panzer units outflanked and broke the Allied lines. Armor had to be thickened as new guns were introduced, and this greater weight called for more powerful engines and more careful design to present as small a target as possible, while offering a good glancing surface.

An American tank, the Pershing

BRITISH MILITARY SWORDS FROM 1600

The seventeenth century saw the beginning of uniformity in the design of military swords, but still nothing emerged that could really be called a regulation pattern. However, certain types were associated with special groups of soldiers, and one of the most spectacular was the *schiavona,* used by the Schiavoni, a group of Balkan mercenaries who served the republic of Venice. This was a broadsword, with a distinctive hilt in the shape of an elaborate basket which varied in detail but basically was made up of a number of wide, often engraved, bars. Pommels were of an unusual shield-shape with an embossed center decoration, often a lion's head.

Many privately purchased military swords were engraved or etched with the cutler's name and often his address as well. Off-duty officers frequently wore a type of sword known as a spadroon; this was very simple, with a straight, double-edged blade and a plain, curved knuckle-bow.

1. & 3. *schiavonas,* late seventeenth century; 2. Dragoon's sword, early eighteenth century; 4. spadroon, late eighteenth century

Scabbards were of leather or, more rarely, wood covered with leather, until the appearance of the 1796 pattern sword for the Light Dragoons with its steel scabbard. Most scabbards were suspended from a waist- or shoulder-belt by means of a hook on the sheath or by straps clipped on to rings on the scabbard. Since swords were purchased en bloc from different suppliers, it is quite possible to find that examples of the same pattern sword differ in detail. Many blades were imported from Germany and then mounted in Britain. As a symbol of rank British army sergeants in the infantry carried a halberd, until the practice was abolished in 1792.

Naval swords were even less standardized than army swords, although a spadroon-type weapon with a carved, five-ball motif on the knuckle-bow was quite common. When the shell-guard was introduced the part on the right-hand side of the hilt, nearest the wearer, could be folded down to let the weapon hang straight. Many had a stud at the top of the scabbard to secure the sword and prevent loss.

1. Infantry sword, and 2. officer's small-sword, both mid-eighteenth century; 3. & 4. cavalry swords, late eighteenth century

British infantry in the eighteenth century carried swords as well as bayonets, the two being suspended from a cross-belt, but it was found that most infantry had little use for their swords, and so it was decided to retain the bayonet only. In 1768 an official order abolished the infantry sword except for officers and for Scottish troops, who retained their broadswords. Swords of infantry officers were, as a rule, straight-bladed, although some were curved. They had to conform to regulations, but as they were purchased privately by the officers there were often minor variations.

There was a great vogue for decorated blades among officers during the eighteenth century, blueing and gilding being especially popular. Blades were also frequently engraved or etched with the royal cypher, military patterns, and mottoes, less often with the regimental badge, name, or number. Many bore the maker's name. Obviously it would have been disastrous to lose a sword in battle, and consequently most of them had a sword-knot, a leather loop which could be slipped over the wrist as a safeguard. The sword-knot was secured to the sword by looping it through a slot or ring on the hilt.

At the end of the eighteenth century most infantry officers carried the sword usually described as the 'pattern of 1796', with its straight, narrow blade, simple, twin shells, knuckle-bow, and a pommel shaped like a classical urn. A new order of 1803 introduced a curved, wider blade and a far more elaborate cast knuckle-bow which, in the case of ordinary infantry officers, incorporated the royal cypher; for officers of the Light Company there was a bugle horn below the cypher. This pattern lasted until 1822 when the so-called Gothic hilt was introduced; this had a knuckle-bow from which other bars sprang out to sweep around and form a simple hand-guard incorporating a circle which held the royal cypher. The blade was slightly curved and had a pipeback, a thickening running along the back edge. The basic pattern of the hilt remained unchanged until 1892 when, in place of the looped, Gothic hilt, a simpler one of sheet steel was introduced.

The shape of cavalry swords was very much a matter of function; thus the light cavalry troopers carried a fairly light sword with a curved blade and a stirrup hilt. This pattern, introduced in 1796, continued in use until the 1820's. The sword was carried in a steel scabbard with two carrying rings mounted on the back.

(*Opposite*) hilt details of: 1. 1831 pattern; 2. broadsword (*c.* 1850); 3. 1796 pattern; 4. & 5. swords of flank officer (*c.* 1810) and heavy cavalry officer (*c.* 1800). (*Below*) swords: 1. 1803 pattern, infantry officer; 2. 1827 pattern, naval officer; 3. bandsman (*c.* 1850)

Infantry officers' swords remained straight, and in 1892 the guard still carried on ceremonial occasions by British Army officers was introduced. It was steel, decorated with a pattern of scrolls and loops which incorporated the royal cypher. With its rather sharp edge the guard was uncomfortable to carry on the belt, and in 1895 the inside edge was curved to reduce this discomfort.

A new pattern sword for general officers was introduced in 1831. Tradition has it that the style was based on a sword the Duke of Wellington brought back from India; certainly the hilt resembled that of the Persian and Turkish *shamshir,* a curved sword. The blade was slightly curved and was fitted with a simple cross-guard, each quillon terminating with a small knob. The grip was straight, with a sharp, forward curve at the top and a hole piercing this section to take the sword-knot loop. Sheaths of black leather with gilt mounts were

(*Left*) 1. a German Imperial Navy sword; 2. a mid-nineteenth-century band sword; 3. the Gothic hilt. (*Opposite*) 1908 cavalry sword: 1. hilt detail, showing the well-designed grip; 2. engraved bowl on the officer's model.

used for formal occasions, but for service wear the scabbard was much more serviceable, being made of brass.

Special bodies of troops did not carry standard-issue swords, those of bandsmen were far more decorative. Hilts were often of brass, but sword designs varied from regiment to regiment, some regiments producing their own modified patterns more by custom than right.

Apart from the Japanese officers who used their swords in World War II, swords have long ceased to be serious weapons of war; certainly most infantry officers discarded theirs as so much useless lumber as soon as there was any action.

Although the cavalry had long been considered an army's main striking force and had played a dominant part in many battles, the introduction of firearms helped to render it obsolete. It lingered on until World War I but was really out of date by the late nineteenth century. There were continual discussions about its role and about its weaponry. Lancer regiments were introduced after Waterloo, but the majority felt that the sword should remain the cavalry's main weapon. There were arguments, however, whether the sword should be used for slashing or thrusting. The verdict was in Favor of a thrusting sword with a long, stiff blade. Known as the 1908 pattern, the new sword had a yard-long blade, a full bowl and for the guard and, most important of all, a well-designed grip that was comfortable and shaped to bring the sword when grasped automatically to the 'charge' position. The scabbard was of steel and suspended by two rings at the top. Unfortunately the sword was 300 years too late for effective service!

1

2

AFRICA

African weapons are of great variety. In the north and along the east coast, Arab influence was dominant. In Somalia and along the Mediterranean coast to Morocco, there is a variety of light, curved sabers. Daggers tend to follow the *jambiyahs*, almost L-shaped blades with highly decorated scabbards similar to those of Yemen. Further inland, from Sudan to Nigeria, there are long, straight swords with handles somewhat resembling European medieval weapons. However, these swords very often have leather-covered grips with a flat leather piece instead of a pommel. The blades are often decorated with etched verses from the Koran. From Ethiopia come the great sickle-like swords called *shotels* with plain horn grips, though straight swords are also used.

Spears are used all over Africa. They range from the short-bladed stabbing spear, the *assagai,* of the Zulu to the long-bladed spear with equally long ferrule used by the Masai of Kenya. Leaf-

Oddly shaped blades of Sudanese and Congolese daggers contrast with simple cruciform swords from the Sudan and the Sahara.

form spears are used in Somali and Uganda.

Special mention should be made of the multiple-bladed throwing knives of the Congo and the superb copper-handled axes of open wrought iron work of the Bakuba chiefs. Smaller, plain-bladed hatchets are common all over Africa and are used for cutting brush rather than fighting. The tribes of southeast Africa also use a throwing club with a solid wooden head, the *knobkerry*, while the pygmies use elaborately barbed arrows which are often poisoned.

Shields are almost always leather but range in size from the large, painted oval shields of Zulu and Masai to the small, round bucklers of Somali horsemen. Armor, usually chain armor, was used by the Hausa, Ghana, and Mali kingdoms. Patterns generally followed Arab designs. African iron was used since about A.D. 100 but too little research has been done on African weaponry to assign tribe and date to the tremendous varieties of forged weapons discovered by the European colonizers.

(*Top*) still popular in the Middle East, the *jambiyah* or curved dagger with scabbard and belt. (*Right*) African spears

NORTH AMERICAN WEAPONS

Indians of North America used clubs and broad-bladed flint knives as their main fighting weapons. With the coming of the white man, Indians quickly acquired a taste for their iron knives and light hatchets. Many of the handles were Indian-made and decorated with porcupine quills or hair, and the scabbards were even more lavishly embroidered. Some of these knives had European blades; others were converted from files or other iron tools. During the seventeenth century, the plain hatchet was converted into the tomahawk, a pipe and axe combination which served the woodland Indian for all needs on the trail. Bows, both simple and compound, existed, but the emphasis on touching the enemy as a sign of bravery (counting 'coup') prevented them from being used much in warfare. Lance-heads of European as well as local origin were often attached to war clubs.

In the late eighteenth and early nineteenth centuries, the introduction of the horse on the Great Plains turned Indian tribes into some of the finest light cavalry in the world. The horse warriors fought with a stone- or iron-tipped lance or

American weapons of the 19th century; Bowie knives on the right.

with a short leather-covered round shield. Although the bow was used, the Indians often carried a long-feathered stick to touch the downed enemy.

On the northwest coast, in Canada and Alaska, some wooden armor, possibly copied from Siberian sources, was worn. The Aztecs of Mexico wore cotton-quilted armor and carried shields, javelins, and obsidian-edged clubs. The bow was not used, but javelins were propelled by spear-throwers, or *atl-atls*. Except for a few knives, no complete Aztec weapons have survived.

British troops serving in North America and such units as Rogers Rangers quickly adopted the tomahawk. In 1759 it was made standard for the Royal American Regiment (60th Rifles). Swords were made for the American revolutionary forces in the 1770's, but where possible, Americans bought European, especially French, blades.

Possibly the most famous of all American knives is the Bowie. This knife had a broad blade with a curved section cut from a thick edge which is then sharpened to give what is known as a false edge. Hilts were of bone, silver, or inlaid with mother-of-pearl.

Designs of American sword-hilts did not differ greatly from equivalent European styles

147

ASIA

Japanese swords

Swords of Japan have always been highly prized and are considered by many collectors to be among the finest in the world. Japanese metal workers achieved an extremely high degree of skill and knowledge and succeeded in producing blades which combined all the most desirable features, for they were stiff without being brittle and had an extremely hard edge. Manufacture was a long and complicated process requiring great skill in hammering, shaping, and quenching. After the blade had been shaped and tempered it still required hours of

(a)

(*Opposite*) 1. & 2. infantry officers' swords, the second an early twentieth-century pattern; 3. an *aikuchi*, or small dagger; 4. a *wakizashi* or short sword, with decoration detail (a); 5. a *tachi*, or long sword. (*Above*) *tsuba*, sword-guards, were often decorated.

polishing, and the resulting mirror-finish on many swords is still as good as ever after five centuries. Many blade-makers signed and dated their products on the tang.

The Japanese warrior, or *samurai*, used several sizes of swords, all basically the same in shape and general appearance. Blades were normally slightly curved and fitted with a wooden grip which was usually covered with fish skin and an intricate braid lacing. Beneath this lacing were two tiny ornaments of metal, *menuki*. Guards, *tsuba*, were almost always rectangular or circular. These flat metal plates were decorated with skill and delicacy: they were sometimes pierced with patterns or else chiseled and overlaid with precious metals.

Scabbards were generally of heavily lacquered wood and those of shorter swords had two slots, to hold a small knife, the *kodzuka*, and a skewer-like implement, the *kogai*, for arranging the hair. Swords were venerated, but in 1876 the Emperor forbad the wearing of them and, as demand stopped, the craft nearly died out. During World War II swords of the traditional pattern were mass produced, but some officers had family blades mounted in regulation fittings and carried them into action.

A few of the great variety of Indian weapons: 1. & 2. *khandars,* often used in two hands; 3. a *pata* or gauntlet sword; 4. a *shamshir;* 5. a *katar;* 6. a complex parrying and thrusting knife

Indian weapons

Indian edged weapons were always far more varied in design than those of Europe and, in such an enormous area as the sub-continent, this is hardly surprising. Some appear to be over-elaborate and impractical but, as most have a long history behind them, they must have proved their worth in battle.

Whereas certain parts of India tended to produce weapons peculiar to one district, the *talwar* was a sword found over a great part of the continent. It was generally, but not invariably, curved to a greater or lesser degree and had a flat disc pommel and simple cross-guard, occasionally connected by a knuckle-guard. Some *talwars* were fashioned completely of steel, but gold and silver inlay were commonly used. An unusual sword was the gauntlet sword, or *pata,* which was held by slipping the hand and forearm into a gauntlet and gripping a bar. The *pata* was used largely as a lance. Scabbards were made of wood covered with various colored materials.

For really hefty swings the Indian warrior used a *khandar*, which was a straight-bladed sword with a reinforced blade and an extension to the pommel in the form of a bar that enabled him to take a two-handed grip on the hilt. Maces were also popular with martial India. Daggers were produced all over India, and many of them were first-rate works of art; probably the finest were those with jade hilts. The jade was carved into animal heads, and precious stones were occasionally inserted for the eyes. Blades tended to be curved, although the *peshkabz* was normally straight-bladed, with a strengthening rib at the back edge.

Peculiar to India was the *katar*, or punch dagger, a miniature version of the *pata*. *Katars* had a hilt with two bars which were gripped in the fist, and the blow was delivered like a punch. Axes were less common, but some superbly decorated examples were made. Occasionally European swords were decorated in gold with typical Indian inlay work. Indian soldiers often wore armor and, although mail was retained until quite late, some plates were also used for reinforcing.

(*Left*) seventeenth-century axe of outstanding quality, decorated with gold and rubies. (*Below*) European weapons, such as this small-sword, were often decorated in 'oriental' style.

Among the least attractive weapons of India were the devices of secret and stealthy attack, and one of the most unpleasant was the tiger-claws. This vicious instrument had a number of curved steel claws fixed to a steel bar fitted with two rings, through which the first and fourth fingers slipped. It was used to give a lethal, multiple slashing wound, usually delivered with an upward sweep of the hand.

Eastern armor

Armor in the Orient developed along differing lines from that in Europe, and there was more emphasis on mail and mail combined with plate. Helmets were not dissimilar in some aspects from their European counterparts: many Indian and Turkish examples have sliding nasals like those used on burgonets of the seventeenth century. Indian and Turkish body armor was usually of mail reinforced by plates, which were frequently highly decorated with inlay. Chanfrons and horse armor of quilted fabric were worn, although most seem to have been composed of small plates with interspaced mail. Occasionally elephant armors were used. Shields were often used, particularly in India and her neighbors.

Elephant armor, possibly from the Battle of Plassey (1757)

Japanese armor was always of outstanding technical quality, and the warrior caste and frequent wars ensured its development and improvement. Most armors were composed of large numbers of lacquered metal plates laced together — lamellar armor. Helmets were fitted with very wide neck-guards, and the face was protected by a metal mask. Japanese smiths sometimes copied European styles, but on the whole Japanese armor retained its individuality.

Although Indian and Japanese arms and armor were of very good quality, those of China were almost always of poor steel. Swords had inferior blades, and design, as in the two-handed executioner's sword, was almost crude. One exception is the pairs of swords decorated with brass and tortoise-shell.

(*Right*) Indian armor composed of plate, fabric, and scales. The helmet has three sliding bars as well as mail to protect the lower head. (*Left*) tiger-claws (nineteenth century)

(*Above*) Chinese executioner's sword. (*Below*) *kindjhal* from the Caucusus

153

Unusual weapons: 1. a *chakram,* the steel quoit of the Sikh; 2. an Indian horn dagger; 3. a giant *talwar,* used as sacrificial weapon; 4. & 5. *kris* from Indonesia, the second with a rare kingfisher hilt

ODDITIES

Some weapons do not easily fall into neat categories, and one such is the *chakram,* which was a weapon of the Sikh. It was a flat, steel ring with a sharpened edge, and the warrior carried six of these quoits around his arm or around the top of his conical turban. It was said that, spun around the finger and then released, the revolving ring could strike down an enemy at 80 paces.

From southeast Asia came the *kris,* which was popular in Malaya, Bali, Java, and other islands of the East Indies. It was fashioned in two basic shapes of blade: one which was straight, tapering to an acute point, and the other with a number of waves in it. The grip was set at an acute angle and the weapon was used to thrust rather than slash. The blades are unusual in that the surface is left rough, whereas on most other weapons it is treated and decorated in a variety of ways. A few of the weapons were ceremonial or votive rather than warlike and had extra large, decorated blades.

Feeling the more blades the better, some sword-makers fashioned weapons with two or three blades. *Katars* were sometimes so made that, as the two holding bars of the hilt were squeezed together, the blades opened out into a trident-like weapon. Less obvious is the purpose of the two-bladed dagger illustrated here, which was carried in a double sheath. As the blades are narrow and close together its advantages are obscure. This dagger appears to be of Middle Eastern origin.

Another development was the dual-purpose weapon, such as the parrying shield of India, which had a small, round shield fitted with two iron-tipped horns so that not only could blows be parried but they could also be given. The scissors dagger was another dual-purpose weapon; it was literally a pair of scissors that could, when closed, be used as an effective stabbing weapon. Many of these appear to be of Spanish or Middle Eastern manufacture. Some daggers were disguised, like the Japanese war fan which looks like a closed fan but is, in fact, a sheath and dagger.

Middle Eastern twin-bladed dagger

Scissors dagger from the Middle East

GLOSSARY

Armet: a close-fitting 15c. helmet fitted with visor and moveable cheek-pieces.

Ballock dagger: 14c-17c. dagger with two lobes at grip base.

Bodkin: skewer-like piece of cutlery used in skinning and preparing of game.

Buckler: small, round fist-shield used in sword-play—often fitted with central spike.

Burgonet: 16c.-17c., light, open-faced helmet with peak and cheek-pieces.

Cabasset: 16c. helmet with pointed skull and flat, narrow brim.

Caliver: light musket.

Chausses: leg defenses of mail, common from the mid-12c.

Cinquedea: Italian sword with short, acutely tapered blade, popular in late 15c. and early 16c. Traditionally five-fingers wide at top.

Claymore: 16c.-17c. two-handed Highland sword. Later, name of Scottish broadsword.

Cranequin: 15c. geared device for spanning or winding back string of crossbow.

Cross-guard: attachment at base of sword- or dagger-hilt, designed to protect hand.

Cuirassier: heavily armored cavalry of 17c., armed with pistols and sword.

Estoc: 16c. sword with strong, narrow blade designed for stabbing.

Ferrule: metal shoe fitted at end of lance or pike staff.

Garniture: group of armors decorated *en suite,* comprising field, tilt, and occasionally horse armor.

Goat's foot lever: simple but ingenious arrangement of levers to span crossbow of medium power.

Hauberk: long-sleeved coat of mail usually reaching to knees.

Knobkerry: club with long, thin shaft and rounded head, used by Zulus.

Lames: metal strips forming part of flexible armor.

Matchlock: system of ignition for firearms, using slow-burning match.

Partizan: long-bladed spear with short, twin, curved lugs at base.

Pauldron: shoulder defense made flexible with lames—left often slightly larger than right.

Pillow sword: light, small, rapier-like sword with single hilt—supposed to have stood by bed.

Pot: popular name for simple, wide-brimmed helmet worn by 17c. pikemen.

Rondel: round plate fitted at the back of an armet.

Spanish morion: *see* cabasset.

Windlass: capstan-like device for spanning crossbow, worked by ropes and pulleys.

BOOKS TO READ

Warriors and Worthies. Helmut Nickel. Atheneum, 1969.

Arms and Armor. Vesey Norman. G. P. Putnam's Sons, 1964.

Catalog of Armor in the John Woodman Higgins Armory. Stephen V. Granescey. Worcester, Massachusetts, 1961.

Miniature Arms. Merrill Lindsay. Winchester Press, 1970.

Arms and Armor, 1930–1450. E. Wagner, Z. Drobna and J. Durdik. Prague: Artia, 1957.

Guide to the Collection of Arms and Armor at the Metropolitan Museum. New York, 1968.

A History of Weapons of the American Revolution. G. C. Neumann. Harper & Row, 1967.

Warrior to Soldier 449–1660. A. V. B. Norman and D. Pottinger. London: Weidenfeld & Nicolson, 1966.

The Armourer and His Craft. C. J. ffoulkes. New York: Benjamin Blom, 1967.

The Archaeology of Weapons. R. E. Oakeshott. Prager, 1960.

Arms and Armour. A. V. B. Norman. Putnam, 1964.

Arms and Armour of the Greeks. A. M. Snodgrass. Cornell University Press, 1967.

PLACES TO VISIT

Before visiting a museum, check that the armor is on display at that time and when the museum is open. Many museums other than those listed here have single pieces or small collections of armor and bladed weapons. Check with the curator to see what your local museum owns.

Metropolitan Museum of Art, New York City.

John Woodman Higgins Armory, Worcester, Massachusetts.

Milwaukee Public Museum, Milwaukee, Wisconsin.

Forest Lawn Museum, Glendale, California.

U.S. Military Academy at West Point, New York.

George Walter Vincent Smith Art Museum, Springfield, Massachusetts (Oriental Armor).

Cleveland Museum of Art, Cleveland, Ohio (Severence Armor Collection).

Mobile Art Gallery, Mobile, Alabama.

Detroit Institute of Art, Detroit, Michigan (Hearst Collection of Armor).

The Mariners Museum, Newport, Virginia (Naval cutlasses, pikes, etc.).

Wadsworth Atheneum. Hartford, Connecticut.

INDEX

OTHER TITLES IN THE SERIES

The GROSSET ALL-COLOR GUIDES provide a library of authoritative information for readers of all ages. Each comprehensive text with its specially designed illustrations yields a unique insight into a particular area of man's interests and culture.

NOW AVAILABLE

MA